Be Yourself

— The Art of Stepping Up —

Nicky Kassapian

BALBOA.
PRESS

A DIVISION OF HAY HOUSE

Balboa Press books may be ordered through booksellers or by contacting:

Balboa Press
A Division of Hay House
1663 Liberty Drive
Bloomington, IN 47403
www.balboapress.com.au
1 (877) 407-4847

Print information available on the last page.

ISBN: 978-1-5043-0157-2 (sc)
ISBN: 978-1-5043-0158-9 (e)

Balboa Press rev. date: 03/14/2016

Contents

This book is dedicated to the freedom of all sentient beings
In loving memory of Peri

Preface

A lotus flower breathes opens, pulsating like a heartbeat. The outer leaves, pushed from the centre, expand and contract by minute degrees just visible to the naked eye. Gradually expanding enough for the next layer to unfold, inhaling, exhaling, expanding and contracting, until the heart, held deep within the flower, presents itself in all its wonder to the waiting the world. We are like the lotus. We open from the inside out.

To create the space for such a phenomenal opening in another being, is an honour and a privilege. It is this which is my inspiration. Empowering others to bloom is my motivation.

I have written an inter-disciplinary book at a time when specialization is celebrated. At such times we can forget how to join the dots together and see only part of the picture. We are multi-faceted beings, so joining the dots together, covering a multitude of topics, can be helpful from time to time. Each chapter can stand alone, yet there is a thread that runs through the whole. I have referred to many sources and included a bibliography, for those who wish to study some of the particular aspects of the topics in more detail.

The book is autobiographical and the names of clients have been omitted or changed to protect their privacy. I have chosen to use the phrase, all that we be, rather than, all that we are, for the energetic quality and feel of the phrase is different. All that we be, reflects our presence. All that we are, reflects our status. Be

Yourself -The Art of Stepping Up - is about stepping more fully into our presence. I have chosen to use the pronoun we more frequently than you for that is inclusive of my journey, as well as, the journeys of others. May it be of some help to you on yours.

Acknowledgements

I would like to express my gratitude to everyone and to everything that has played a part in my life. Teachers every single one and all bearing teachings and gifts, if only I take the time to see. Whatever that part has been, I know it is that which has made this work possible.

My heartfelt thanks to my god parents Brian and Millicent Spiller who encouraged the creative within. Thank you to Millicent Spiller, who kept asking me about the book I was writing, years before I had actually started to write it. Thank you to my parents for giving me this precious life and to my brothers for coming in to be with me. Thank you to Randy Kwei, who delivered the message write a book during a conversation in an airport departure lounge. Thank you to Jeremy Haw, who reiterated the message write a book and supported and encouraged me all the way. Thank you to John and Karina Stewart for inviting me to work in the sacred space they have created. Thank you to Marc A. Cornaz for all the sound advice and encouragement. Thank you to all the clients who have trusted me, opened before me and still asked me to write a book.

Thank you to Mireille Lefevre, Deborah Carlyon, Lucia Posari and Rebecca Walker, for their patience, feedback and support, and their tireless eyes. Thank you to Jason White and Julia Chow of Connixon Rewards, for their assistance with graphic design, and to Paolo Righetti for taking the portrait. Thank you to Anne Barcelona for being so efficient and making sure I completed the steps necessary to go to print. Thank you to many others for their on going encouragement.

Finally thank you to Peri, my guiding light for so many years. The most incredible teacher, mentor, guide, friend and companion, anyone could ever ask for.

To the Reader

What was it that prompted my desire to be myself, step up and take personal responsibility? I had been cruising along through my life, doing what I thought I was meant to do and being what I thought I was meant to be. All this in hindsight, was generated by my own sense of inadequacy, self-doubt and the core belief pattern of not being enough. That meant I had opened the door of manipulation, coercion and persuasion.

Then one day, triggered by a breaking of the heart, as I stumbled and fell, I realised I had not a clue about whom or what I was. From that moment on I decided I wanted to operate from a place of self acceptance rather than self-criticism, personal responsibility rather than blame and enjoy interdependency rather than codependency, so I undertook to go on a mission to get to know this "self" a lot better. When we step into self-worth this results in trusting ourselves, using our voice and allowing ourselves and others to be who we truly be.

Years later, as I began working with others, I noticed and continue to notice, that we keep coming back to the same things. As beings we share commonalities by just being on the planet. Many experience a shifting sense of identity, fears, love and loss. We experience judgements, inadequacy and discrimination, as well as, change and work. Trust, grief, and joy, shock, desire, and resistance are also part of our human experience. So are forgiveness, acceptance, and compassion, shame and vulnerability. We experience guilt, relationships, blame, and break ups, death and birth. These common elements are the ingredients of life and how we respond to them creates the life we experience.

Frequently we are navigating these commonalities alone, without guidance or tools. All too often we may feel as if we are floundering and drowning in the moment of life, lost and unsure. We do what we can to make the best of an already deeply challenging situation.

What follows are integrated chapters, drawn from parts of my own walk and the gifts, practices and techniques, which I have used along the way. They are brought together here, as possible ways to support others as they move along their own spiral of life. They are practical, easy to follow and simple to do. Each chapter has been created so that we can clear, centre and connect to our innate nature more deeply, emerging regenerated and transformed, ready to be a catalyst for effecting change in the world to which we return.

This is a beginning and a sharing of things that worked for me, as I began to consciously and deliberately navigate my spiral of life. As I did so, I began to reveal myself to myself and in doing so I opened more fully to others and to life. I found it was essentially about pausing and looking at oneself.

When the Mind no longer needs to be held
And the Spirit is cradled in the open-heart
We are as golden moots of inspiration
Bursting forth into creation
Extending far beyond imagined limitations
To a place of peace transcending all understanding
This is where Life begins and Love resides

Nicky Kassapian © 2008

One

The Art of Stepping Up –
It's All Coming from You

We like to think that the world is coming *at* us.

It is not.

The world is actually coming *from* us.

In taking responsibility for ourselves, we accept that our lives are in our own hands. Only then can we make the changes that will change our lives. This is when we transform. This is when the world we experience begins to transform. When we are all doing this, it will be a very different world.

In shifting our view of the world from being a victim of it, to being an active participant in it, self reflection and inquiry, courage and integrity, perseverance and a healthy sense of humour are essential. This shift also requires deliberately and consciously choosing to operate through the matrix of love and stepping beyond the matrix of fear. In life we are faced with this choice continuously, and the commonalities we all experience as human beings, are in fact our greatest opportunities to exercise this choice.

A matrix, according to the second definition in the *Concise Oxford Dictionary* is "an environment or substance in which a thing is developed" or "a womb."

Initially our human form develops in the womb and we take on the external environment sensed through our mother and internalize it as our own. (Sills 1947, 61). Then, with fluctuating awareness, from birth until death, again and again, ad infinitum, we continue to develop in the environment in which we find ourselves.

The matrix of love, in brief, appears to be an environment of acceptance, personal responsibility, allowing and trust. It creates sensations of space, unity, freedom and peace. It honours inter dependency.

When we view the world as coming from us we are in communion with the world and All That Is. By operating through the matrix of love, we move *with* the world. We move towards others and our authentic selves. Our communion nurtures our innate nature and consciousness. This transforms our experience of the world, the world we experience and the "us" the world experiences.

The matrix of fear appears to be an environment of judgement, restriction, limitation, blame and doubt and it creates the sensations of contraction, separation, pain and suffering. It thrives on codependency, as we relinquish personal responsibility and attempt to make others responsible for our happiness.

When we perceive the world as coming at us, we separate from All That Is and we interact with the world largely through the matrix of fear. We separate from others, moving away from them under the guise of disappointment, and this disconnection feeds our neuroses and global unease.

Observations of the world illustrate all too clearly, how we are encouraged to operate through the matrix of fear. There has generally been less encouragement for operating through the matrix of love.

As a result, it seems we are rapidly forgetting that we are so much more than we believe ourselves to be. We are something at our very core that is so pure, so free and so intrinsically perfect that we appear to have become a mystery unto ourselves.

We are human beings having a spiritual experience. We are spiritual beings having a human experience. We are pure energy manifesting in something we label as human form. We are intrinsically connected to nature and it mirrors back to us, again and again, that which we be.

When we disengage from what we really are, we disconnect from the heart and identify ourselves with what we have, what we do, and who we know. None of that is us. It is our armour, and it keeps us at a distance from the fullness of our lives, the fullness of our being, and the fullness of our connection with each other and ourselves.

We spend so much time looking outside ourselves for validation and approval, for how to be, what to do and what to have, that we become riddled with self-doubts and indecision. We create and operate through a fabricated identity and our energy gets all tied up with trying to hold on to it and protect it.

When we doubt ourselves, we lay ourselves open to manipulation, coercion and persuasion. At times we find ourselves on the receiving end, and at others we are the ones manipulating, coercing and persuading. It is little wonder that we find ourselves in a world where our voices seem to go unheard. We have stopped using them as we have disengaged and disconnected from our true nature.

Yet in order to take personal responsibility for ourselves and to be ourselves, we need to look at who we think, perceive and believe ourselves to be. In accepting that the world is coming from us, we also need to look at our projections of whom and what we think, perceive and believe others to be.

For us to mirror back to nature that which it is, we are called upon to drop out of our heads and fall into our hearts. We are called upon to engage with life and with each other more fully. We are also called upon to disengage from our all-too-convenient shields of disconnection.

What if all we need to do is actually look inside ourselves for a while?

We are no different from nature. We are in fact nature expressing itself in a human form. Just for a moment, remember that we come into being just like seeds in nature come into being. The seed becomes a sprout. As a sprout pushes its way through the earth to the surface, what shows itself first is the tip of the shoot. As it unfurls, there are two leaves joined like wings, and from the wings emerges a single primary leaf or heart. After the heart comes the main stem, the leaves and the roots, connecting it to the earth.

We are the same. Our very inception is a miracle and our conception, a collision of energy in space. Those seeds, an ovum and sperm, that merge and find a secure place to grow, transform into an embryo. Nine months later, if there is a natural birth, as the baby with its mother's help pushes its way out into the world, it appears head first. This is followed by the arms, and from these emerges the heart, and from the heart, the torso, the legs and the feet, connecting us in turn, to the earth.

At our very core, metaphorically speaking, we have wings, followed by the heart. Our shoulder blades and arms are reminiscent of wings. We are, in essence love, angels coming into land. If only we could perceive that everything in the world is emanating love, starting with ourselves, what a different world we would be experiencing and creating.

Even though we may be emanating this as new-borns, the world around us is all too often emitting a different message. This happens if we are born into societies and communities that are governed by the matrix of fear. Beliefs, thought patterns, identities and behaviours, are activated and quickly incorporated into the perceptual field of the new arrival and imposed upon what was once definition-less awareness.

The wings and the heart, overwhelmed by layer upon layer of viewpoints counter to our innate truth, seem to disappear. They are however, lying low deep within.

How can we touch back into who and what we be?

This requires showing up and embodying the body, dropping out of the head and into the heart and really allowing ourselves to touch the earth, grounding and connecting.

We can do this by building a sacred relationship with ourselves, one that expresses reverence for our lives and moves us from ego to essence . To live life is to feel life, to taste it, to vibrate with it, and to colour everything we touch with it.

This only happens when we are actually present and in the body. To begin to move beyond the matrix of fear and into the matrix of love, so that we can move towards the world and others, we need to embody our bodies more fully and traverse our spiral of life with awareness.

We can consciously and deliberately begin to traverse our personal spiral of life, deconstructing the facades we have put up, taking off our armour and putting down our shields. As we do this we will find ourselves on an experiential journey to a place beyond the visible world and who we think we are.

Be yourself. This is where the art of stepping up comes in. Only you can do it. Others can support you by showing up, by being true and by sharing their experiences. However, only you can decide what is right for you. Essentially, the key is pausing and looking at yourself.

Life is an offering, and I offer that which I have been given, that which I have received, and that which has been revealed, as the knowledge of the heart. Take from it that which speaks to you, and allow yourself to give birth to yourself.

Two

The Spiral of Life

A spiral symbolizes the movement from which all things come and into which all things go for rebirth and regeneration. The spiral is not about upwards or downwards; it can be viewed as horizontal. Everything depends upon our perspective, as does everything in our lives. We are creating though our perceptions and compounding them through our responses.

I see life as horizontal and circular rather than vertical and linear. For ease of description I see it as a three-dimensional horizontal spiral, which when looked at from a different angle, is a series of concentric rings, and it is these which create the spiral.

When we are born, we all come in on our own particular point within the spiral, and that could be anywhere on any one of those rings. From there our spiral of life begins and continues in the physical form. Where we land is simply dependent upon what we have decided to integrate in this particular incarnation.

There is a flow, a dance if you like, where movement back and forth from one ring to another, occurs. At times without completion of the circle and in a seemingly random way, yet it is perfectly designed for the evolution and growth of the being. It is allowing what needs to happen to happen, as and when it needs to happen. This randomness of motion creates the perfect space for the next piece to unfold.

We store all our experiences along the spiral of life, and as we collide with one experience and everything associated with it, with conscious deliberate awareness, the imprint of it will then pop from that very origin point within the psyche. The emotional, mental, physical and spiritual bodies, all pop and recalibrate in unison. It's a bit like the collision of atoms, they blow each other apart and space remains.

If, for example, part of our mission in this incarnation, is to dissolve and integrate the core belief pattern of not being good enough, then we will navigate the spiral of life in order to dissolve and integrate that particular concept. No matter where it is located, no matter what form it takes, and no matter how many lifetimes it has been there.

In terms of the human psyche, speaking from my own experience, I notice that there are various types of shifts which can occur. Change seems to occur when we recognise patterns, and we deliberately address them. Transformation occurs when we drop them from automatic. Absolute transformation is total, and the imprint is gone. This occurs when the origin point, everything in between, including the current embodiment, collide, coalesce and pop all the way along the spiral.

An absloute transformation, which maybe a rare occurrence, moves us beyond or back to what we truly be. Rare though it is, we can become proactive in preparing the ground, through conscious awareness, and supporting deliberate change and transformation within ourselves.

As you traverse your own spiral of life, exercise your discernment, and apply that which assists you to step beyond the matrix of fear and into the matrix of love.

Breathe in love and breathe out love.

Three

Breathe in Love, Breathe out Love

The Book of Love

'*Once upon a time, long, long ago there was a child wandering through the luscious grass and vibrant flowers, singing with the birds, which were flying right beside her. There was only nature and her in this enchanted garden, where the colours and light, created rainbows and stars, and endless flowers of life. Everything was radiating love. Every blade of grass, leaf, petal, beetle, ant, bird, dragon and butterfly, were pulsating with love. All the fruits in the trees and all the vegetables in the earth were also emanating love. Even the stones and water in the stream and the particles in the air were singing with love. Space itself was vibrating with the very essence of life, that essence being love.*'

I used to wonder what the world would look like if everything was emanating love. What would the world be like if we could all see that the world is radiating love? On some level, I know that it is, and all it takes is a change in perception to be able to see it. Once we see it, we can celebrate it, feed it, nurture it, and give it the space and the freedom to grow. In turn it feeds and nurtures us, giving us space and freedom to grow, in all our myriad of ways.

Tuning into nature, looking into the sky, into the water or into the leaves, any element will reveal itself, reflecting back to us, exactly where we are. What an incredible gift of love that really is. Coalescing to reveal ourselves to ourselves, from the inner realms, which are so often obscured by the business and busyness, of the external realms. Ten or fifteen minutes in nature everyday, gives us insights into where we have been. It shows us where we are, and raises the question of where we would like to be.

A common experience is to walk or drive down a street. One morning everything we perceive looks drab, dead and desperate. The next day, the same street looks funky, vibrant and expressive. The following day, the same street looks artistic, inviting and colourful. No matter when we look at the street, it is still the street. It is us who have changed. If we make it a deliberate conscious intention, we will find beauty no matter where we are, no matter how we feel, no matter what is going on in our lives.

Beauty is beckoning to us every minute, every second of life and within this beckoning, is the doorway of love. It is the path to the enchanted garden. This is a way to create paradise. It is already here, right here, right now, and all it requires, is a shift in our perception. And this shift, this altered state, requires our willingness, our determination and our courageous perseverance. All that lies within us. It is free for us to tap into and activate, anytime, anywhere.

What if every view we have of ourselves just isn't fixed or real?

What if everything we view everyone and everything else as, just isn't fixed or real either?

What if we can move through whom and what we think and feel we are, into space beyond the restrictions placed upon every moment?

What if it is actually easy to do?

Take a moment and contemplate the following.

What would the world look like, what would it feel like, what would it be like, if everything was emanating love?

What would we be like, how would we be treating ourselves and our fellow beings if everything, including us, was emanating love?

So having become so disconnected from who and what we are in truth, how do we get back?

Try this for a few minutes. As you inhale, imagine you are inhaling love. As you exhale imagine you are exhaling love. Ever so gently, breathe in love and breathe out love, breathe in love and breathe out love. See if you can do it for a minute or two, with full concentration, and feel what happens.

I dropped into this space, without thinking one day, and the experience took me by surprise. Later I practised deliberately, and here are some of the things I observed.

I noticed that at first the head kicks in and tries to define what love is, and then the question comes, how do I do that? And just as quickly the questions fall away as the system, the innate knowledge, the inner wisdom being, knows exactly what it is and how to do it. No explanations necessary, just breathe in love, breathe out love, breathe in love and breathe out love. Whatever happens for you, enjoy it as it is in that moment, as your own experience. Each time it can be different, and for each person it can be different.

The next thing is that our perception of the self and the world around us might begin to soften. Things may begin to fill out, to become more fluid, and everything may appear to take on a luminosity which was invisible before. Vibrancy may enter into the field of perception, depth may become visible, and the light may seem to have an almost tangible quality.

What has changed? Simply the perception we have been operating through, and that changes everything.

The simplicity of such a practice allows truth to be revealed, through the experiential clarity we experience. This is a step towards consciousness waking up to itself. Of realising it is simultaneously everything and nothing, and that the Infinite is also everything and nothing. They are one and the same. We are one and the same. Breathe in love and breathe out love.

If it is this simple, and we've just seen that it is, how come we have been missing it for so long?

Well on an immediate level *we like to think that the world is coming at us*. That is a convenient get out of personal responsibility, and a get into victim consciousness. However, *it is not. The world is actually coming from us.* I heard this repeatedly during a Buddhist meditation course, and it has stayed with me. In the context of the class, it was referring to the concept that the world we experience, is coming from the ways we have treated ourselves and others throughout all time.

The idea that the world is coming *at* us, which has been compounded through our social environment until it becomes a belief, is neatly flipped on its head just by breathing in love and breathing out love. Suddenly we can feel that the world is coming *from* us. This very statement contains such a wonderfully delightful perception shift, that it can open us to the possibility of transformation.

If our experience of life and the world changes, oh so subtly, simply through consciously and deliberately breathing in love and breathing out love, then we are having immediate confirmation, proof if you like, that the world is actually coming *from* us. This is a direct refutation of the most common and prevalent core concept of the fear matrix, whereby in victim consciousness, we think the world is coming *at* us. Relinquishing responsibility, maybe why we have we forgotten how the relationship between the 'I' and the world actually works.

On a deeper level Michel Odent, in his book *The Scientification of Love,* and Robin Lim in her book *Placenta the Forgotten Chakra,* are among a few in their field, who have conducted extensive research, to show just how great an impact birth and the way it is conducted, has upon the newborn, the mother, and ultimately upon society and the world as a whole.

To quote Michel Odent, *"In most known societies, until now, it has been an advantage to moderate and control the different aspects of the capacity to love, including love of nature, and to develop the human potential for aggressiveness. The greater the need to develop aggression and the ability to destroy life, the more intrusive the rituals and cultural beliefs in the period around birth have become."* (Odent 2001, 28)

The way we arrive on the planet, has a significant effect upon our lives our connection to ourselves and to each other. There are times when a caesarean is called for in emergency situations. Even in such cases, much can be done to preserve the sacredness of the process of birth, and the vitality of those entering onto the planet.

It has been shown that the natural hormones, which are released in the body during the birthing process, create the interconnectedness between beings, in this case the mother and the child. Oxytocin is commonly known as the love hormone, and it forms the foundation of connectedness. It is, along with a natural cocktail of other hormones, released during labour, relieving the mother of the pain, and flooding the pair with Oxytocin. The mother and baby are naturally taken into an altered state of being, one of unconditional love.

A significant impact of a lotus birth, which involves leaving the umbilical cord uncut, and allowing where possible, the baby to make its way up the belly to the mother's breast, is that it activates the heart, and this creates the foundation for interdependent relationships. The newborn experiences two hearts beating as one, its own and its mother's. Whereas inside the womb, it was as if only the one heart was beating. Everything from the mother came to the embryo, including feelings, thoughts, bumps and so forth.

Franklyn Sills, in his book *Being and Becoming*, documents extensive research on the embryonic stages, and the physiological and psychological effects of those stages upon 'ourselves.' It seems we internalize them as our own, and later manifest them externally once we are born on to the planet. The Ecole de Somatopathie, methode M.R.P, have observed that the nine months prior to our conception, the nine months of our development in the womb, and the first nine months on the planet are pivitol periods.

The cutting of the umbilical cord, before the baby has had a chance to experience the two hearts beating separately, is shocking. It is an abrupt separation, triggering reptilian brain activity, namely flight or fight, in one who is vulnerable to all the elements. Not only is the activation of the heart important, so too is the ignition process, and this occurs as the baby passes through the birth canal and out into the world. The third ventricle in the brain is activated, and results in potency within the baby being stimulated. This is our drive to live life to our upmost potential. Without potency our life force is low, and our motivation to develop is sluggish. It is rather like being stuck in second gear all the time. The ignition process and activation of the heart can fortunately be stimulated later, through craniosacral therapy or cranial osteopathy.

It is apparent that our passage from pre conception through to the hours, days and months after our birth, has a profound effect upon us, and is fundamental to our unfolding life.

It is interesting to note, there are increasing numbers of elected Caesareans occurring throughout the world, and increasing numbers of victim conscious concepts arising. In relation to the whole birthing process and elected caesareans, it may be a sensible wisdom to ask, "elected by whom and why?"

As victim consciousness is being expressed, and taking hold across the globe, we begin to see the breakdown of social communities, more and more destructive dysfunctional relationships, codependent behaviour, and on a national level, greater conflict and wars.

Increasing the levels of separation and disconnection at birth, results in a greater sense of disconnection and separation in individuals. Touching into our innate nature acts is a counter balance to this. Intuitively speaking, all the signs are there. The evidence, is already presenting, on all levels, in societies all over the world.

As we continue through life, past those first moments of existing independently from our mothers, unless very fortunate, we are bombarded with stimulation, encouraging us to become further focused on a contracted existence. Disconnection continues and inquiry, along with self-expression, experiencing feelings and trusting the intuition, are less encouraged. Roles come in thick and fast, and games with ever changing rules, leave one in a state of confusion, unearthed, and doing what everyone believes one has to do in order to survive.

Generally this continues unquestioned until some event, circumstance or trauma, in our lives creates that pause. That is an opportunity to step back from our life, to step out of the known, and really take a breath. Sometimes we are medicated through it, which can have a numbing effect on our capacities. For those who observe that pause, and then dive into the opportunity created by the events, or for those who simply wake up one day and say "umm this doesn't work for me anymore," then begins the beautiful, delightful adventure and discovery of who you be.

This disconnection from ourselves, our interdependent relationship with one another, the planet and All That Is, has brought us to the place where we find ourselves today. As with so many times before, we have a choice to continue on or to press pause, to take a breath, to step back, and to consciously and deliberately take a different course.

We could choose a course, which is in harmony with the knowledge of the heart, and with the geometric patterning of the very essence of life, where, as depicted in the *Flower of Life*, everything is interconnected. Everything is energy, even empty space is energy filled. There is nothing which is devoid of energy.

Remembering that, we too are energy within a form, may help to visualise the similarities between all beings, all things, and gradually allow more fluidity back into our lives. Scientists in the physics world discuss this at great length. Nassim Haramein, through The Resonance Project Foundation, illustrates our interconnectedness and interdependence, not only with each other and everything on the planet, but with the entire universe.

How can we begin to retrieve and nurture the essence of who we really are?

We can build a sacred relationship with ourselves. One way to do this requires that we make and take, time and space for ourselves every day. This creates the opportunity for us to touch into our true nature, and drop into ourselves, every single day.

This is something we do when we free ourselves of distractions. The distractions we interact with most of the time are; the television, the computer, the tablet, the phone, food, drink, magazines and newspapers. On a more subtle level the distractions of gossip, day dreams and fantasies. It is just as important to take and make, time and space from these things every day, as it is from friends, family, partners, children, pets, colleagues and so forth.

All the distractions above, allow us to zone out of the here and now, under the disguise of being busy or occupied. That is our collective self-deception.

Generally we create and hold on to distractions, out of fear. Fear of feeling something or not feeling something, fear of being something or not being something. Whatever it is, we are in resistance to something, and as long as we avoid it, it will stick to us like glue. Once felt, it dissolves, and then we are at liberty to experience something other than that which we have been in fear of. Then we may just start revealing more of ourselves to ourselves.

Start with five minutes a day. This is a manageable minimum for most people. To my knowledge, creating time and space for oneself, alters the way life unfolds.

Allow your eyes to be open, so that you can be present in the here and now. Where possible, touching the ground, so you can connect to the earth, sit or stand somewhere, and just be in that space with yourself, in silence.

Place your attention loosely on a point in front, and observe when you wander off, or when you are no longer aware of your focus. This gives an indication of when we are zoning out, whereas, the intention is to be present in the here and now, in a gentle and relaxed way.

From putting my attention loosely on a point I can notice my thoughts as they arise, and when I find myself getting caught up in them, I label the thoughts, so that it frees me to come back to the point. Perhaps I simply say to myself "thinking, thinking, thinking" or "worrying, worrying, worrying" or whatever it is that I am doing, and magically I return to the moment, and my attention realigns once more.

Become conscious of the breath. Follow it for a while, going in and out of the nostrils, down into the lungs and the stomach, and then up into the head centres and the brain. Connect with the comings and goings of life through the breath. That can bring insights and openings from deep within.

Next close your eyes and be inside for as long as feels right. Perhaps take a moment to wish for the good health and happiness of others, or for someone you know who is experiencing struggle in their life, or for specific areas in the world that are in conflict, and finally to the planet and to yourself.

In gratitude open your eyes and take a few moments to contemplate the day ahead. Set an intention if that feels appropriate.

Some days it is easy, peaceful and calm. Other days it's a challenge to even find a point, let alone track the breath. I stay there none-the-less, for I am showing myself where I am in that given moment, and that is an invaluable gift. I become aware of my presence no matter what's arising, and that means I am more able to touch and drop into myself. Each time, I become more aware of layers that obscure the innate nature. This gift arises when I allow myself the time and space for it to reveal itself.

The beauty of the practice is that we can do this anywhere. When we go to the gym, we can make it part of our programme, to be conscious and present in the body, without the distractions of the music or the television. When we drive, we can be present with the motion of driving. When we do anything, we can experiment with being absolutely present with whatever we are doing, just for five minutes at a time. The inner shifts may be profound, and the external world will shift right alongside them.

As we touch into our authentic selves, more deeply, we may begin to reflect on, whether the world we live in really has to be the way it is. The relationship we have with ourselves contributes to the external world we experience, and it is possible for things to change. The technology is available, and as a collective we do have a choice.

Collaborative consumption and collaborative economies may well be the answer. They are starting to blossom all over the world. They are examples of where technology is being aligned with the purest essence consciousness of presence, unity, interconnection and love, for the benefit of all. They are built on trust between strangers, and the primary currency is reputation. *What's Mine is Yours: How Collaborative Consumption Is Changing The Way We Live* by Rachel Botsman, presents valuable and interesting food for thought.

How do we create a world where all beings are seen as equal, where all beings are cared for, respected and valued? Where all beings have clean water, nutritious life-giving food, and where the system of exchange becomes one of value and service? It seems the world in which we live no longer needs to be the way it is.

At a very grassroots level, I've heard of a construction project where everyone was paid the same. The developer found the mid-point of all the salaries, and then gave that to everyone involved. The project went smoothly and the outcome was very positive.

Ultimately it's really very simple, and it begins and ends with ourselves. All we need to do in life, is to be, give and receive love, without expectations. That is the key. That means to ourselves, to others and to all things animate and so called inanimate. This is child's play. A child knows this. Yet we have been encouraged to disengage from the feeling world of energetic connection to everything, to move out of the intuitive innate knowingness, guided by the expansive authenticity of the heart, and to move instead, into the head and the limitations of control.

Touching into our innate nature, allows us to find our place in the world. Exploring how we define ourselves, allows us to show up in the world more fully.

How do you define yourself?

Four

Definition – Know thyself Better

How can it be, that you are going along very nicely one day, where everything is going according to plan, and then the next minute, "eeeekkkkk!" you are pulling the emergency brake cord, and doing whatever you can to get off the train. This happens when you wake up and find yourself riding on the train called my life, yet it is a train you do not recognise. You can't figure out how you got to be there, nor can you quite believe it. In fact everything about the train and you, seem to be a mismatch. That leaves you feeling confused and lost, and very definitely disorientated. In some cases, it may even seem as if someone else has pulled the emergency cord, and pushed you off the train. Then you struggle for a while, trying to get back on, yet you realise it's not right for you anymore.

Plans are frequently based on expectations, and expectations are based on a story we have told ourselves, or a story others have told us, and we have taken on as our own, believing it to be true. We aspire to fulfil the story about how our lives should be, in terms of education, work, income, having our own house, a family, a car, a profession and so forth. The stories all seem to have achievement deadlines as well. The thing is, plans are simply plans. They are not fixed. Plans are always changing, just as we are.

When we look at the story closely enough, we see that this story is layer upon layer of expectations. In truth, very little of it may actually be real, relevant or in alignment to who we actually are, moment to moment. Even more accurately, it is far from who we be, at the moment of the rhetorical question, "what am I doing on this train?"

Traversing the spiral of life, back to what we really are, is a hoot when you can keep a sense of humour. Especially as we get to explore just how amazing we are as creators, and what it is that we decided to create for ourselves. Usually it consists of limitation upon limitation, so that our world view has become so defined, that if something occurs to challenge that defined space called; me, my life, my work, my family and so on, a rather uncomfortable sensation of unravelling occurs. We can feel as if our whole life is deconstructing before our eyes.

We lose a sense of who and what we are, and feel somewhat confused, lost and unsure of life, un-trusting of self. Frequently we can become more cautious of others. The tendency is to grasp onto anything that is familiar, or that may still be solid, even if it causes pain, further suffering, or death. The classic saying "better the devil you know than the one you don't," is a wonderful example.

This is a wasteland, and it is here in this land that everything can unfold, expand and transform. The question is, are we willing to allow that to happen? Are we willing to be a conscious aware presence within that unfolding, or are we going to go into resistance and fix on whatever we can, so we can keep things the way they were, no matter what?

I did this, the resistance that is, for at least a year after the event, which became the catalyst for me pulling the emergency break to stop the train. The event was the completion of a five year relationship. The realisation that I had lost myself, came through in bits and pieces, over the next few years, and by then, there was nothing left for me to hold onto.

Change is happening every second within us, and externally to us. There are few constants in life, yet one of them is change. Another one is us. We are constantly changing. Given that change is actually one constant in life, it is an act of self sabotage when we pretend that things are fixed, and we fixate on whether change will really be good for us. Change in turn, becomes something more feared than embraced and celebrated. Think about change and watch where your thoughts take you. Feel the energy that you have around the concept of change. Feel it in your body.

Why does it bring up fear more often than joy? We have become so attached to things being the way they are, that when they change, it means we change, and that could mean all sorts of unknown situations arising. How will we know what to do, how to be, and indeed, who to be? This triggers beliefs we have around getting it right, and being enough.

We forget that that unknown can be anything. So isn't it time to make it the best thing we can?

Step lightly and willingly into the vastness of space, and start to discover what you have been creating all this while. A great place to start is from definition. Take time to note and digest your answers. They may surprise you, as much as they surprised me, when I decided to really have a look at who this "me" was.

Who am I?

What am I?

These two questions alone can trigger journeys into familiar and unfamiliar lands. They are key unravelling our own mystery, to our being authentic, and they are key to our freedom.

Ask yourself

What do I do?

Who am I in relation to that?

What would I be without that role or that work?

Ask yourself

Who do I know?

Who am I in relation to them?

Who would I be without that role?

Ask yourself

What do I have?

Who am I for having those things?

Who would I be without those things?

Can I be that, even though I do that work, I know those people, I have those things?

Can I be in the world and not of it?

Can I make it a practice to remember that all the definitions are not who I am?

I am not what I do.

I am not who I know.

I am not what I have.

Having, knowing and doing less than others, does not make me a lesser being.

I am not what I don't do.

I am not who I don't know.

I am not what I don't have.

Having, knowing and doing more than others, does not make me a better being.

Recognising that none of this is what we are, might just make our existence lighter, better and freer of the pain and suffering that resistance and desire often creates.

Limitations are definitions imposed upon pure awareness, which lead to limited perceptions, viewpoints and identities. This creates restrictions, which in turn create greater contraction, pain and suffering. Where there is only increasing contraction, pressure builds, until there is an explosion, blowing everything apart. Destruction and annihilation occur. Whereas when there is harmonious balance and a flow of expansion and contraction, as in a torus, the results are an increase in the flow of energy, creation and evolution. The torus shows us how energy moves in its most balanced and dynamic flow process.

The most important thing to remember about definition is, that changing the way we define ourselves and changing the way we define others, changes the way we experience our lives and others, and it changes the way others experience us.

We are not what we think we are. Or rather, we are not what we have been conditioned to think and to believe we are.

We are not what we do.

We are not who we know.

We are not what we have.

We may nod our heads in intellectual agreement with those statements, but how often do we really take them on board?

Many of us wait for a major event to happen before we begin exploring these notions. It doesn't need to happen as a result of an earthquake, a tsunami, a financial meltdown, a death, a war, a divorce, a heartbreak, the loss of the job or an accident. We can start to take stock of who we are, without being pushed into it. We can do it right here, right now, and it will take us exactly where we need to be. The key is to start looking at how we define ourselves. As everything actually begins and ends with us, starting with ourselves is the best place to start, for that is what we know. Or is it?

The way to get back to a semblance of what we may be in truth, is to divest ourselves of what we have been imposing upon space, within the container we call the body. What follows is a practical exercise, which will take you beyond your current perception of self. I did this after a particularly intense week of critical self talk. Finally I had had enough and decided to look at how valid everything that I was telling my self, actually was.

Simply put and simply done you can keep it personal and make it fun. Take some paper or a book. Start by writing down the first words that come when you think about yourself and how you would define yourself. Write down how you would define yourself on all levels, which means physically, mentally, emotionally and spiritually. Allow this to take place over three consecutive days. You will be amazed at how many words come up. Stay out of judgement, censorship and have no tormentor. Be compassionate.

rite, include the opposites if they arise, the strange,
1 the wonderful. Include all the things that come
up, and be compassionate with yourself during the process.
For example, many of us define ourselves through initially a
name, Nicky, and gender, female, and our position within the
family, daughter, sister. We also define ourselves by our work, our
profession, our emotions, our country and so forth.

When the list is done leave it for a few days, making additions
only if and when they arise. At the end of the week, review the
pages, suspending as much judgement and critique as possible.

First delete any double ups.

Second circle any you find most helpful.

Third highlight in a different way all the ones you find
limiting or you dislike.

You will then be left with any that are neutral. Indeed you
may even be left with a blank space.

How comfortable is it to be in the neutral or blank space?

Breathe in love, breathe out love, breathe in love, and breathe
out love. Trust, receive, believe, breathe in love, and breathe out
love. Allow the unknown space to envelop you. Allow yourself to
become more aware of how you perceive your existence.

Now look at the definitions you wish to keep and ask yourself
why? How do they assist me in who I am, and in what and who
I wish to be? Do these definitions serve to support me, or do they
get in the way of me being all that I can be?

Next look at the ones you wish were not there, the ones you
resist, or find impeding and ask yourself why?

Examine each one carefully and decide if you wish to let every
aspect of it go, or whether there are some aspects you wish to
keep. You can create a ritual and burn the ones you feel no longer
serve you, if you wish.

It is a good time to reflect on what serves you, and perhaps
add some definitions that will assist the future you.

Just bringing conscious awareness to the definitions and
doing this practice, will begin to dissolve those which no longer

serve you. The self perception will shift and change as a result. When we can see it, we can choose to continue to operate though it, or to stop. It's a choice.

The gift of this practice is that it gives us a snapshot into what we have been imposing upon ourselves. It subsequently creates a space where we can decide whether we still wish to operate through all of those definitions, or whether we wish to be more selective and discerning about what we are imposing upon the space that we relate to as "us" or "me".

This technique made me realise just how cluttered and full I had become. At the same time I realised how redundant, harmful and sabotaging, many of my definitions were. Some I had created myself, some I had taken on from others. All were my responsibility. This practice meant that, for the first time, I could really look at and see what I was creating and perpetuating as me. That meant I now had the power to change it.

Simply by becoming aware of the myriad of ways I was defining myself opened the pathway for change, if I wanted to follow it. First I needed to see it then, I could chose to stop it and finally move into something different. I looked at those definitions I wished to keep and asked myself why? How do they assist me in who I am and in what and who I wish to be? Do these definitions serve to support me or do they get in the way of me being all that I can be?

I reviewed the ones I wished to be rid of and examined them more closely, to see if there were any aspects I did actually want to keep. For example, with words like *stubborn*, *wilful* and *ego*, I realised that I could retain the constructive elements. Stubborn has the energy of inflexibility, perseverance, determination and strength. Wilful has the energy of drive and motivation, and a strong sense of self. Ego has the energy of motivation and arrogance.

I decided to let stubborn go, yet hold onto the qualities of perseverance, determination and strength. I did the same with wilful and ego, retaining motivation, remembering without it little gets done. The beauty of this technique is that we can see who we have been being, with all our contradictions and multifaceted natures. Then we can decide what we'd like to put into the space of "me" and become that. It really is that easy and effective.

As I looked at the definitions, it began to dawn on me that many of them were generated by fear rather than love. Another important insight we gain from examining our self definitions is just which matrix we are predominantly operating through, fear or love.

As beings, we operate principally through the matrix of fear or the matrix of love. Whichever one predominates, we define ourselves by, and experience our life in accordance with it. This takes definition to a whole other level. I was astonished at how much unconscious fear was present in many of my definitions.

I mean, I was both *interesting and boring*. I was *useless and not good enough*. I was *loving*, yet I was *unworthy and invisible*.

As I have asked myself, and the clients I work with, on countless occasions, which matrix are you operating through here? To do that effectively of course we need to be aware of the components of each matrix and that comes in the next chapter.

I was so critical, judgemental and hard on myself, while being more supportive, tolerant and easy going towards others, it was crushing. For others I felt I could operate through the matrix of love, for myself I operated through the matrix of fear, unable to see that I too am a work in progress, just like everyone else.

This is why it is so important to build a sacred relationship with ourselves. One that is kind, compassionate, forgiving, nurturing, loving and celebratory.

After this, I spent a month writing myself a daily love letter. A friend told me about the practice, which they had read about somewhere. I haven't been able to track it down and my gratitude goes to the person who came up with it.

I wrote as if I was writing to a lover, celebrating aspects of my personality, physicality, senses, creativity, emotional expression, my humour, my mind and so on. I found beautiful paper and cards to write the letters on. Sometimes I would invite myself on a date, like going to an art exhibition, or for a walk by the river.

I posted each letter to myself once a day, numbering each envelope or postcard, and as they began to be delivered by the post office, I'd read then in numerical order. When I received the invitation I would then go and do it. It was a sweet and heart centred thing to do.

Until we can truly give this to and receive this from ourselves, we will continue to doubt the fullness of it, and on some level mistrust it when it comes from others. Unless we can give this to ourselves, we get in the way of the flow of love from others towards us, and on some level, the authentically present and unconditional flow of love, from us towards others.

The following question applies to every aspect of our lives.

The matrix of fear and the matrix of love, which one are you choosing to operate through?

Five

The Matrix - Fear or Love

As human beings we tend to operate through two primary matrices, fear or love. We frequently chose one over the other.

The matrix of fear expresses itself through the following attributes; control, lack, guilt, victim, blame, hope, limitations, restrictions, contractions and low self-esteem. It also shows up in a sense of separation, self-doubt, shame, judgement, resistance, desire, comparison, obsession, conflict, attachment and stagnation. It creates the dynamic of an ever shrinking world, where rigidity and fixation abound, creating increased pain and suffering. Victim consciousness and codependent relationships seem to thrive.

The matrix of love expresses itself through the following attributes; trust, allowing, acceptance, forgiveness, compassion, intelligent regret, gratitude, altruism, unity, possibility, responsibility, as well as, balance, innocence, creativity, vulnerability and non-attachment, and it creates fluidity of movement, space, freedom and peace. Personal responsibility and interdependent relationships seem to flourish.

Much can be added to each matrix. The closer we look and the more we clear, the more extensive the lists become. However in essence, the above covers the common aspects to a more immediately tangible and workable degree.

As we examine how we define ourselves, in combination with other beliefs that we are engaging in, holding these two matrices in our awareness, helps us to become much more aware of who we are, what we are doing and how we are doing it. Most importantly we can gain valuable insights into how to change it.

I am sure many other people have noted these two primary matrices, yet I had not heard anyone else talk about it before, and when I share it with clients, for many it is an eye opener and a game changer. It transformed a lot for me.

I attended a silent retreat for seven days, and it gave me an opportunity to look more closely at just how much I was imposing upon myself and allowing others to impose upon me. While I was there I realised I had never truly seized the day. I had been doing so called "brave and courageous" things, but they had been coming from an assertive space. It was to prove I was not afraid. In fact, beneath that asserted identity, was fear. Fear of being weedy, fear of being a scardy cat, and fear of being a girl. Subsequently the insight arose that I had been carrying this fear since inside the womb.

I began to understand a little better, why I had struggled so much as a child, with what I felt to be true about the world and with what I was told was true about the world. It was a matter of which matrix was predominating in the belief system I found myself in.

The view I held, and still hold, is that life doesn't have to be the way it is. It applies to so many things. People do not need to be starving anywhere in the world. Fear is the driving force behind so much of the world we currently experience, and if all the effort that is put into conflicts was put into dialogue, war would not need to happen, and vast inequality would no longer be the norm.

Jose Mujica, President of Uruguay, stated the following in his inaugural address to the UN September 24th 2013. *"$2 million dollars per second is spent on military budgets around the world every day, while medical research enjoys a mere 5th of the military budget."* (Mujica 2013) If the money spent on wars was spent on helping and feeding people, if it was invested into clean water and safe alternative energy sources of solar and wind, instead of on weapons, then none of the man made suffering would need to happen. In fact a better life could easily be supported.

The world is our mirror. Not only is it coming from us, it is also a reflection of us. Whatever is showing up, is showing up and telling us something. The more we can take the time to look at it, to listen and learn from it, the more rapidly we and the world can transform.

If we shift the way resources are distributed and allocated, if we change the way we perceive the world, if we start to think as a collective, things could be very different. I was told, like so many others, that I was being unrealistic, idealistic, and irrational and that it was impossible.

There is a way and there is how. Globally we are being asked to touch into ourselves, to look at what is really important for us and to start acting locally and globally, for the highest good of all. From collaborative commerce, community and entrepreneurial initiatives, we can see the way and the how in action. The key is to do it responsibly and with integrity, without sowing seeds, which we may not wish to harvest later on.

The matrix of fear may well be why many cannot see that things could unfold in a different way. It may also be why there is so much conditional giving.

Conditional giving is not giving, it is control. Conditional love is not love, it is control. Conditional sharing is not sharing, it is control. Anything that is conditional is a form of control, either on an obvious or subtle level. Control is an aspect of the fear matrix. It is through this that many of us have been brought up, and to varying degrees, we continue to operate through it. We often miss, that underlying the need to control, is a sense of our own inadequacy or lack. Control is a key element in codependent relationships.

A deeper analysis and increased awareness of the matrix of fear and the matrix of love, was one of the significant things that made me sit up and pay attention. A more in-depth examination of these primary matrices shows us that they are the antithesis of each other.

The Matrix of Fear

The matrix of fear encompasses restriction, limitation, control, separation, contraction, guilt, blame and victim consciousness, to name but a few attributes. The world shrinks, breathing becomes laboured, the body starts to shut down upon itself, anger and violence increase, sadness deepens, schisms multiply, divisions widen and protectionism, dogma and distortions expound, and permeate everything. It results in extended and exacerbated pain and suffering.

It is very crafty and it employs lack as its greatest ally. Lack is a false myth and encourages the attribute of greed. When we stop operating from lack, we shall stop operating from greed. It is then that we can begin to create a more authentic, harmonious and balanced environment in our lives and in the world as a whole.

The affect it has on us, is that personal and collective responsibility is often relinquished, rights are reduced, victim consciousness and a "what's in it for me?" attitude prevail. Critical appraisal, discussion and thinking diminish. Diversity shrinks, homogeneity thrives and with that monopolies grow bigger and bigger, though fewer and fewer in number. The distribution of wealth remains in the hands of the few, and the abuse of power appears to extend further and further.

The truth becomes skewered, and the lives of many are increasingly manipulated, to such an extent, that there is little or no time to stop and listen for what is actually the truth. When humanity becomes too busy on a day to day basis, to lend a hand to those in need, when it becomes too busy to hear the call of a neighbour or to help another, when the palm of our hand seems to have merged into the latest small gadget, we have lost our way. When the server crashes and we fall into depression or feel as if the whole world is lost, recognise this as a signal. We are losing our way. When obtaining the latest in thing is more important than taking the time to thank the assistant or help another, then it is a sure sign that humanity has well and truly started to lose its way.

Our way is being dictated to us via the things we have, the things we do and who we believe ourselves to be. Yet we are so much more than all the stuff we are persuaded to accumulate and encouraged to emulate.

Many aspects of these are controlled by elements outside of us, which are also operating from the matrix of fear, and keeping us busy enough, distracted enough and focused enough on immaterial, material things. This frequently means we do not have the presence, the time, the energy or the motivation to stand up for ourselves, for others, for the truth, for humanity, for animals and for the planet itself.

Yet, we do have the capacity to care for each other. Each natural disaster sees a surge in humanitarian actions, and our innate desire to be of help and assistance to each other expresses itself clearly. Why are we so reluctant to express that side of ourselves in our day to day living?

How often have we failed to stand up for ourselves, fearing that we lack the power? How often have we failed to stand up for others, fearing that we lack the power to make a difference? How often have we failed to stand up for the truth, being a whistleblower, fearing we will be shut out by our group, exiled from our country or imprisoned? How often have we failed to stand up for humanity, animals and the planet, fearing we lack the power to do so and to make a difference?

Globalisation is actually resulting in a reduction of diversity. There is the appearance of there being more choice for the consumer, but in fact, if you look at the supermarket shelves in countries around the world, you will see that they are all stocking the same goods.

Biodiversity is being reduced through agricultural trade agreements that require all fruits and vegetables to look a certain way. Food producing conglomerates appear to be doing what they can, to control the production of food, through the seed banks they have created. Even when this control has been shown to destroy the health of the agricultural land, the insects and the people they are claiming to assist. Multinationals of all kinds, are going to great lengths to maintain control of the natural resources used in their products, including bringing law suits against individuals, governments and in some cases against entire countries. This is fear based.

Countries relinquish responsibility for their actions and harm other countries. In turn, a country may relinquish its responsibility of due diligence, and by doing so, allow itself to be harmed. The external world is a reflection of ourselves, and if we really take ownership of our desires, we will begin to realise that such behaviour is also coming from us. Where are we looking for the best advantage, being economical with the truth and ignoring the consequences of our actions? Where do we allow ourselves to say yes because of the money and forget to read the small print, only to cry unfair after the event?

Human beings are being coerced into believing that they need to look a certain way, to be right, to be perfect and to fit in. The increase in cosmetic surgery is a case in point. Electronic gadgets, and the advertising sales pitch that goes with them, are a further interesting example of where lack plays an important part. If we don't have the latest version we are out of the in crowd, we are lacking in some way, be it in style, kudos or wealth. Whatever it is, we are lacking. Our manipulated desires are having a detrimental effect on the planet and all living on her. This is causing greater and greater destruction moment by moment, and it is all driven by fear.

When we are operating through the matrix of fear it impacts upon everyone in our sphere of influence. One of the most interesting things I have observed from my own self reflection of growing up and watching children being brought up in the world today, is how quickly and readily we are taught to disconnect or disengage from our feelings, from our intuitive knowing and our innate wisdom. How rapidly we develop self-doubt and mistrust of our own guidance, preferring instead to hand it all over to someone else. We are so ready and so quick to relinquish responsibility for our own experience and to dis-empower ourselves, which in turn means we also dis-empower others.

A child will do anything to receive the love and the attention it wants, especially if at any time it feels that love and attention is threatened or maybe withdrawn. Jean Liedloff's book called *The Continuum Concept. In Search of Lost Happiness,* is an example of just how possible it is to bring children up in a way that encourages their sense of self, and allows them to find their place in a community. At the same time, allowing the community to function in harmony with its members and its environment. To have our worlds revolve around the child, and or to be allowing a child to control our world, is out of balance. It is possible to apply many of the fundamental behaviours Jean Liedloff observed in the indigenous community. It just takes a little bit of thinking outside the box.

What I refer to here, are some fundamentals to any interpersonal relationship. I look at children, for it affects their later relationships. If we are attempting to care for and protect our children via the matrix of fear, we are going to continue to create the world we are currently experiencing. If we are unethical in our dealings with our children, we will experience more abuses of power and manipulation in our world, for we are doing just that. We are creating it. Our relationships with animals are just the same, and for those who have a pet or animals exactly the same ways of behaving apply. They are energy just as we are. They are simply showing up in a different form.

To blatantly lie to a child in order to get the child to do something, is condoning the practice of dishonesty. To say "don't go into the water there's a shark in there," in a place where there are no sharks, is one such example, or "watch out there are snakes over there," when there are none, is another. To threaten and or bribe a child, into doing something from an early age, sets up the pattern of manipulation and generates the fear of loss or lack. Children respond to clear boundaries, just like adults do. We all like to know where we stand.

Children give all of us the opportunity to step up in our own awareness and integrity. They show us our issues, and if we have the courage and the willingness to allow it, we can address what we are projecting and imposing on to others, and appreciate what incredible gifted and wise beings children really are.

Then we will be able to work in harmony with them, creating self confident, aware and trusting people who enjoy interdependent relationships with others, who know and find their place with grace and ease, and allow others the space to do the same.

If you love someone give them everything you have. However, where are you within this equation? Indeed, being absent in order to provide doesn't work for the child. If we are not what we have, who we know or what we do, why would our child be a reflection of what we give it, who we connect it to, or who we are?

A child needs our presence, more than it needs our presents. Children need our guidance and explanations, more than they need our lies, threats or connections. A child needs our love, more than our status. Underneath it all, just like our children, we may need and desire their love, more than anything else.

Channel your energy into what is really important for you in the moment. If that is providing for your child, then bring it into balance every day.

Fear is a choice and it is time to make it a conscious and deliberate choice. If we allow fear to govern the space in between us, we live in confusion, simply increasing the degrees of pain and suffering we are willing to endure.

Living through the matrix of love encourages clarity.

How do you want to live your life?

The Matrix of Love

The matrix of love is unconditional, non sticky compassionate love. This matrix encompasses trust, allowing, space, freedom and peace. It is a reflection of our intrinsic pure consciousness, it is called by some our innate nature, by others supra consciousness. This matrix is unlimited, unfettered and unrestricted. It is in many ways undefinable. It is compassion, love and wisdom, it is without attachment. It is All That Is and it flows through us like the air that we breathe. It enters in through allowing, breathing in love, breathing out love, and surrendering to it. It is the very essence of life. It is us.

If we stop and pause in nature just for a while, what is really important to us will arise very quickly, and then we will know intuitively what is right for us. And what is right for us will ultimately be right for others, especially when it comes from a space of conscious awareness, rather than react.

It is when we try to please others, to second guess or to assume what others want us to be or want from us, that it all goes askew. Us being true to ourselves and showing our true selves, allows others to know us and where we stand. It allows them to know where they stand with us. It gives everyone permission to be their authentic selves, and clarity steps neatly into the frame. Everyone knows and can take their right place with grace and ease.

When we operate through this paradigm an expansion occurs. When the physical structure moves out of fear and into love, a relaxation, a softening and a balancing naturally happens. Equilibrium comes into play and everything seems to be so much more fluid. It's clearer, lighter and brighter, and for some reason there is a grace and ease with which things can unfold. The energy of openness comes into the field, generating a willingness to connect with others, a willingness to be more fully present with whatever is going on, and an ability to hear and to respond to situations in a calm and clear way. Recognition begins to dawn upon us, of the similarities and unique qualities of each and every being, creating and gifting their diversity to the harmonious existence of the planet. The desire to improve remains, yet it is no longer at the cost of another. It is for and with others, so that *all* benefit from the improved skills and practices. Interdependent relationships flourish.

The matrix of love, allows all beings to be valued and respected by each other. Acceptance is a key element, as are forgiveness and compassion. To trust and allow, requires a degree of acceptance and a foregoing of fear. This requires forgiveness of self and others, and this in turn, requires great compassion. Intelligent regret, rather than guilt comes into play in this dynamic.

For example, this is intelligent regret in action. I got angry with a friend because the placement of a certain item had been changed. I recognised I was trying to be Miss Perfect and controlling. I decided to apologise. I then decide I will remove the item and create a new space.

Guilt in action however, might be, I got angry with my friend, now I feel bad and embarassed, I can't see them again because when I do I will still I feel so awful.

Intelligent regret, as I understand it, creates the space so that the action one has taken is owned, with the recognition of what we have done and the impact it has had on ourselves and others. This ownership is followed by the motivation and commitment to take a different course of action in future situations. Intelligent regret frees up the past identity and clears the space for a new unfolding to occur. Guilt in contrast, keeps the past identity locked up in a holding space, and the energy of the event is continually in the field.

The matrix of love allows creativity to flourish. Indeed it is an active component of it. Biodiversity projects such as The Venus Project and other Communities such a Findhorn, recognize this and nurture it. Creativity results in innovation, and when coming from the matrix of love, innovation comes from the desire to improve for all, in harmony with all. That is the people, the creatures and the environment. When this is distorted through a drive and motivation for greater than or more than, purely on a profit basis, it is coming from a space of lack and that, as we know, is the ally of fear.

It takes courage, tenacity and ethics, to constantly come back to operating through the matrix of love. Power, rather than force comes with it, and this power is guided by ethics. As such, it leads in a direction where by life and the world in which we live, can change through consciously and deliberately deciding to co-create rather than to separate.

We are at a pivotal point, as indeed all points can be. However right here, right now, is where we are, and what we decide right here, right now, as individuals affects how we experience the world, how we perceive the world and how we are perceived and experienced by the world. More than that, it affects how we are impacting upon the world, and in energetic terms, it affects what we are projecting out on to the world, which is coming from us in the first place.

Our responsibility is real and tangible. It is not to be given over or left up to someone else. Our responsibility is to create internally, the world we would like or prefer to experience externally. That means clearing up the inner realms, clearing out the clutter, getting into alignment with our greater vision and pulling out all the stops to be present in the here and now. Stepping out of the matrix of fear and stepping into the matrix of love. Stepping beyond who we think we are and into the unknown. It is there that we will find all that we can be, for we are in fact, infinite.

This brings us to how questions. How do we step out of the fear matrix and into the love matrix? How do we drop the habits of a life time? How do we disengage from victim consciousness, and move into our intrinsic nature and consciousness, which is more aware of itself as infinite?

There are of course many answers, many ways and many teachers and teachings, which address such questions. The practices I have shared are a few I have found valuable on my way, and I stress, I am still on my way. I continue to come across processes, insights, viewpoints, teachers, guides, teachings and guidance, all of which assist me in allowing myself to be, operating ever more fully from the matrix of love.

A point to note here are the wonderful sayings uttered by many great teachers and teachings: "The answers you are looking for lie within. Know thyself. Be a light unto yourself. To thine own self be true."

Ultimately we are the teacher, and as such we need to examine our beliefs, our shadows, our self deceptions, and our levels of integrity. Any method, teaching or process that encourages and supports us to be open to discovering the answers that lie with ourselves, and empowers us to uncover the truth through realisations, is one worth looking into more deeply.

I have found that the key is to own and accept that I am creating what I am experiencing, as a result of the beliefs I am operating through. I am choosing to operate through them on some level of consciousness, even if that is on an unconscious one. This means that to truly know myself, to be a light for myself and be true to myself, I will need to examine my beliefs, judgements and self deceptions.

Six

Beliefs - We are what we Believe

What could be worse than not being good enough?

Nothing.

What could be worse than being good enough?

Nothing.

A loop of conflicting beliefs, such as this one, has us locked up tight and heading for a heart attack, burnout or break down, soon enough. This is a lose-lose scenario, and what we lose is our *joie de vie*, our creativity and our zest for life.

Beings get all caught up in conflicting loops such as this one, and so embedded can they become, that life is lived through the loop, without even realising that it is there.

So how do we get out of the loop?

The keys to getting out are:

1/ Self Acceptance

2/ Forgiveness

3/ Love and Compassion

These elements are critical to any move outside of the current way of living. There are additional elements, which also play a significant part; self awareness, willingness, and patience, vulnerability, intelligent regret, and perseverance, courage, gratitude, and allowing, trust, innocence, and action, intention, purity, unity consciousness and recognition.

Here they are listed element by element, yet one without the other falls short. It is together that they form part of the matrix of love. Within it is the energetic field of allowing and trust, which creates space, freedom and peace.

The other matrix, the matrix of fear, which we 'choose' to operate through, is a most pervasive one. It is insidious in the way it infects everyone and everything. This creates constriction, contraction, and separation, restriction, repression, and limitations, the need to control, an ever shrinking world and life view, an ever shrinking life, guilt, shame, and victim consciousness, resistance, desire, hope and blame.

Along with all of that, comes increased pain and suffering on all levels. It becomes hard to breathe, to move or to laugh without assistance in the form of medicine or stimulants, which are in fact largely depressants. As our world contracts, our life becomes more and more of a shadow of anything remotely resembling what being alive actually is. We become the walking dead.

There is another way to live life. There is another way to be and it is simply right there inside of each and every one of us, waiting to be seen. It's waiting silently on the flipside.

It is so close, yet we do not see it and for all I know we may not want to see it. I didn't for many years, afraid of being different, afraid of being the same, afraid in fact of being alive. Far more fun to swim around in pain and suffering, and dream up more ways to create more pain and suffering for one and all, than to simply stop and turn it all on its head.

Suddenly everything looked different. I came out of a five year relationship, extremely disorientated. I had lost my sense of self, and what I was able to touch into I didn't recognize, let alone like. I went on a path of hedonistic self-destruction and oblivion, numbing the pain in avoidance of the shame of having failed to compromise enough to preserve the relationship. In hindsight, thank goodness I had failed, and I say that with gratitude to the partner, who went on to get married to another and have a family.

The break up, the ensuing heart break and hedonistic life style, brought me face to face with someone I did not know. It was a catalyst for me to step deliberately into unveiling, unravelling and revealing myself to myself. It is what brought me to my knees, through examining how I was creating what I was experiencing. It then allowed me to find my feet and to stand up on them. It has been a significant step to where I currently find myself.

At some point, I woke up to the realization that if something in my behaviour didn't change, then something was going to give, and it was highly likely that that something, was going to be me. I decided to take the graceful way to healing, and was fortunate enough to be guided to a course that had as its premise "beliefs precede experiences." I am a big one for personal responsibility, so this appealed to me instantly.

There are many personal development courses with that premise at their core, far too many to mention here. All have their gifts and insights. Books explore the same premise, for example ones by Bruce Lipton, Louise Hay, Inna Segal and Annette Nootil, and numerous others.

The premise that your beliefs precede your experience, means that they act as a filter through which you then view and experience life. Everything, when it comes down to the bottom line, is a belief, even if it is a judgement. Even what I am writing here, they are all beliefs.

I write of my own experience and of what I have witnessed through working with others. Beliefs are a key to transforming ourselves, our lives and the world.

One way to start moving and choosing to deliberately step out of the matrix of fear and into the matrix of love, is to start examining what it is that you believe about yourself and any given situation you find yourself in.

What is a belief? It can be anything that comes out of our mouths, with conviction. Some beliefs we are aware of when we take them on. Many we are not aware of at all. It's rather like having a wardrobe filled with clothes, some are familiar, and yet many we do not recall how they got there or even who they belong to. In fact, our wardrobe is so full, we are finding it hard to squeeze anything new in, as it keeps getting pushed out or covered up by the old. When this happens it is time for some major clutter clearing on the inner realms.

We are all extraordinarily powerful creators, and we like to be right. So whatever beliefs we have about ourselves, even if they seem completely crazy from where we are viewing them now, we will create circumstances, situations and events, and attract people into our lives, who will confirm the very beliefs we have about ourselves. The world really is coming from us.

In all life contexts, I have found that this same concept can be applied over and over again. Whatever we believe about ourselves, about others and the world, we shall experience in our world. When we hit a glitch in any area of our life, this is a signal it's time to have a look at the beliefs we are operating through.

For myself I had done a process called Walk for Atonement from Resurfacing®, (Palmer 1994. 84) on being perfect, well actually on not being perfect. What I found when I got to the end of my walk was that, what could be worse than not being perfect, was actually, being perfect. Why? Well, if I was perfect, I would not need to be here anymore.

It was then that I realised that I actually did want to be alive, living my life fully. Up until that point, I had been doing a lot of things to challenge staying alive, and that could have been because I actually feared life itself. I believed that I was not perfect enough for life.

You see how twisted fear can be? Fear keeps us in a holding position, just like guilt. It stops us from moving on, and keeps us disconnected from the heart and the intuitive centre. It keeps us stuck in the mind chatter or the contracted head centre where things go round and round and round, just like the hamster on the wheel.

If, for example, we run our own business and suddenly things start going less well, we can usually find that we are operating from a self sabotaging belief, which then impacts on everything around us, including what is unfolding in the business. Handle that and the environment you have found yourself in will, rather miraculously, begin to change. It is coming from you.

I worked with a client, who was keen to free himself from the limitations he had placed upon himself and his business. He believed he was not reaching his full potential. The business was merely reflecting his inner world. This had arisen from the fear matrix, and a core mass consciousness belief of "not being good enough."

I asked him to do a Walk for Atonement, so that for every step he was to take, he would whisper something that could be worse than not being good enough. He returned with the realisation that for him "nothing" could be worse than not being good enough. Then I asked him to do a second walk, on what could be worse than being good enough. This time there was a bit of a struggle and eventually he came back and said "all I get is nothing."

A beautiful loop had been created, where by *not being good enough* was just the worst thing, and nothing would be worse than that. Yet on the flip side, at the same time what could be worse than *being good enough*, was also nothing. The cross over points for the two identities, the one who believed it was not good enough and the other who believed it was good enough, was a profound sense of nothing. The resistance to being and feeling this sense of nothing, created the conflict and the struggle he was experiencing.

His life experience vacillated between the two identities, the respective beliefs and nothing. Each time the person had almost reached a point of satisfaction in their business, a self sabotage would occur, virtually reducing things to nothing and then creating the feeling that they were nothing. This meant that they would strive and strive to be better, so much so, that they were unable to even see what they had achieved because it all looked like nothing.

They were working themselves into the ground, going round and round in circles. The recognition of this loop was enough to dissolve it, and to create some space and the willingness to allow and trust. There was just a little bit more freedom and peace. Allowing ourselves to be a work in progress, just like everyone else, is an enormous gift. Allowing it for ourselves, means we then truly allow it for others. If you are not good enough for yourself, then you will invariably make others not good enough for you, on a gross or subtle level, undermining them to prove yourself right.

Another client I worked with, had spent may years doing extreme sports, having accidents, recovering and going back to another extreme sport to repeat the pattern all over again. He stopped talking for quite some time to reflect upon the following question: "have you ever considered that you may actually be afraid of life, given that you continue to flirt with death and tell me that you are willing to die?"

Death seemed to be evading him no matter how hard he tried and yet life, waiting to be embraced by him, was far more of a challenge than any extreme sport he had done. Here the fear matrix was operating below the radar, but it was operating none the less, and in this case the choice was clear. Which matrix do you wish to live your life through, the one of fear or the one of love?

I heard back from this person a few months later, out of the blue, when I was sitting in a place of fear, debating whether to ask if I could become a student of a respected teacher. The client was thanking me for having asked that question, "which matrix do you wish to live your life through, the one of fear or the one of love?" Ironically and beautifully it was my own words being quoted back to me, that assisted me to let go of the fear I was sitting in and trust all would be well.

For the client the extreme sports may well continue, yet the motivation for them can change. There can then be genuine enjoyment, rather than the hidden agenda operating behind the scenes. I used to do extreme sports as well, although I was fortunate to be accident free. So there were, as with many clients, some parallels with my own life.

To thumb one's nose at life and to flirt so openly with death, may well be in order to get back at those you feel have let you down in some way. Anger, sadness, disappointment, and resentment are all facets of the fear matrix too. When they are disowned, buried, forgotten and denied, these emotions, thoughts, feelings and stories, play out in our lives, in the actions we take and in what shows up in our world.

The finding of a core belief or a core pattern of behaviour is such a gift. For most of us it is lying just beneath the surface. At times with embarrassment and shame, at times hiding behind a forceful identity, masquerading as the complete opposite of what we really feel or believe about ourselves. To find it takes courage. In fact to allow ourselves to be ourselves, truly ourselves, takes courage. Operating from the love matrix takes courage, and it is something that all of us have, even if we think we don't. You'd be surprised at just how much courage you have already exerted just to survive on the planet. Read *Daring Greatly* by Brene' Brown, and you will get more insights into just how valuable and interconnected vulnerability and courage are.

When we believe something is difficult, we are setting ourselves up for an uphill journey. We feel depleted if not defeated before we even begin. The body feels heavy and our vision clouds as tiredness sets in and we haven't even begun. Yet if we switch the word to challenging, something delightful happens. The body actually straightens, vision widens and softens and energy flows freely and possibilities appear. All from changing the word we are imposing upon the situation. Miraculous! I saw this happen with a group of students who had joined a six month language course. The director of studies came in to give them a talk about what lay ahead. I was to be their core teacher, so I sat in and listened.

The talk began well enough with congratulations on having secured a scholarship for post graduate studies. Then however, the tone changed, and for the rest of the talk, they were repeatedly told how difficult it was going to be, how difficult it was to achieve the right score in the exams, how difficult it was to study overseas, and how difficult it was to fulfil all the requirements.

I watched the bright open gazes of the students, turn inwards and their bodies, at first straight and tall, shrink and fold into themselves. The talk was over and after a short break I was up front with only one purpose in mind, to reignite the passion that I had seen before the director's talk.

I asked the class how they felt about the task ahead and nodding with slumped postures, they said "oh it will be very difficult." I suggested they close their eyes and take a deep breath and just feel what that felt like. After a minute and a sharing, it was agreed they felt heavy, tired and totally demoralized. I suggested they change the word and say to themselves, "it will be challenging" and to take a breath and feel what that felt like. In contrast they started to sit straighter and widen back in their chairs. The feedback was, they felt more energized and lighter. They all expressed a desire to get on with the task at hand. We made a contract as a group, to focus on the challenges ahead and let go of the notion of difficult.

The gift is that just by changing a word, we can change the energy of our belief, and therefore, our approach to and our experience of a situation. The students went on to do very well, and the director of studies refrained from giving talks focused on difficulty. These students moved out of surviving their experience and started to live it and enjoy their lives.

We can do the same by looking at our beliefs and our definitions. Look at how easily we can make then helpful. For example, *I'm not heard, I'm unlovable* and *I'm not seen*. Just changing them with conscious deliberate awareness to *I'm heard, I'm lovable* and *I'm seen*, begins to create a shift in how we perceive ourselves.

This in turn creates a shift, slowly and surely in how others perceive us as well.

Use this technique for everything that is creating challenges or pain and struggle in your life, and watch as it begins to change. Examine your views towards your work, your health, money, and the people in your life and so on. Take responsibility, take action and shift it from the mind out.

We are focusing here on moving out of surviving mode and into living mode, being truly alive, so that in the longer term we can assist others to live life, rather than to survive life. Life does not have to be a battle all the time. Redistribution of resources, reorganisation of funds, rethinking food, water, health and education, would all mean that life could be lived for being alive. Life could then be enjoyed more, as the precious gift that it is and be celebrated as such, rather than bartered with, bought and sold and survived through.

The gift of recognising, owning and accepting our core belief patterns, are that once we've seen them, so to speak, we can make a conscious choice to keep them or to let them go. Either way we will be doing so with awareness and that in its self, will alter things, even if only a fraction. There will be a much bigger change, if the decision is to let a belief pattern go. Then we can bring our awareness to all the situations, that that particular belief shows up in, and address it. A useful process, shared with me by Andy Shaw is something he called the Spot it, Stop it, Drop it, process.

I have used it to diminish my core belief and behavioural pattern of *not being good enough*. The process works like this, if you can see it, you can stop it and if you can stop it, you can drop it. You simply need to be present and committed to yourself to practice it. I admit that it took me a year to get committed enough to myself, to really knock that one on the head. Once I was committed, within a month of using the spot it, stop it, drop it process it was done. At least, I was done with that point on the spiral of life.

When I finally decided to do it, I was thinking about someone I really liked and I watched as the thought arose "yeah but he wouldn't want to go out with you because you're not good enough". What? There and then I decided I was going to get this one well and truly out of my system. So I spent a month turning it off in every area of my life, from the grossest to the subtlest levels. For example, "I can't wear that because... No one will like me if... I mustn't because then I'll..." and so on. It was amazing, it was fun and it was incredibly liberating to address that layer with such presence.

These beliefs show up everywhere. When we took them on strangely enough, it was for a reason that served us. Yes, even something as debilitating as *not being good enough* served me. In primary school the class was divided into the lower, middle and upper tables. The youngest were on the lower and the eldest on the upper, with all the rest of us on the middle table. Sometimes places would switch, depending on a subject and the perceived ability. I was a fast reader so on the upper table and this meant I was potentially showing up my older friend. I decided to fail so that my friend could succeed. Naturally his success was because of me. The ego surged and that belief of *not being good enough* was all about power. On the surface however, it appeared to enable another to be better than me. Below the surface, a whole different story was going on.

That is my earliest conscious memory of using the *not being good enough* belief, to feel I was better than another. I could now feel good about myself, because I had helped another, and at the same time take away their success, because without me they wouldn't have achieved what they did. I was the heroine and their success was really mine! That logic made the belief, *I'm not good enough* into a power base and that made me, very important. The other person, I hasten to add, had no idea of this heroic action.

Later when I didn't do so well in exams, it got me attention, it meant I was seen, I was worried about, this perhaps, was love. Still later, it would sabotage relationships, as self-doubt and jealousies arose and disconnection occurred. That core belief would also sabotage dreams and my own successes, as I would not even be able to appreciate what I had achieved.

The above practices can be applied to every impeding core belief you hold about yourself. And you can do that without having to go anywhere. Yes, it may help to go and do a self development course. Yes, it may help to have a therapist. Sure, it helps to have the money to be able to access any of those. In reality however, our conscious awareness is all we need, right here, right now to begin to take those initial wonderful steps to reclaiming ourselves. The rest can and will come if we so desire it and if it is needed for our discovery. Do what you can in this moment. It is simple, it is effective and it is fun.

The definitions you noted down from chapter three are all beliefs and they are a good place to start, especially with the more crushing beliefs. Start to approach them with the processes above, and follow them with the questions for contemplation below.

Start somewhere, start with you and start exactly where you find yourself today. Ask yourself

What do I really, really, really want to do?

Followed by

Why can't I do that?

Keep asking that until you crash into your core belief and you will feel it experientially. You will know it and on some level it will feel like a truth to you. Ironically, it's a truth that you hold about yourself, which is crushing you. Sit with it even if the mind wants to deny it, run away from it or resist it. Sit with it, observe it and then decide whether it continues to serve you, or if you are ready to be grateful for all it has taught you. Then start the 'spot it, stop it, drop it' process. There are other techniques such as NLP, *Neuro Linguistic Programming,* or EFT, *Emotional Freedom Technique,* popularly known as 'Tapping', which can also help. Find what works for you and start today. Letting go is deciding to stop holding on anymore.

It's time to be as much of yourself as you can be.

Once we become comfortable with beliefs, it is then possible to see the nuances that occur through our own judgements and projections. They are simply beliefs masquerading in a different form.

Seven

Judgements

"Judge not lest ye yourself be judged"

An old saying, which has much truth and yet another part can be added. That is, realise that when you judge another you judge yourself. Judging a person does not define who they are. It defines who we are.

When we feel that we are being judged by another, realise that this is our own judgement of ourselves, being projected out onto another and then re projected back on to ourselves.

Remember it starts and ends with us, and this can be applied to all areas of life. Step up our participation in and ownership of our lives and what we are creating, and everything will then begin to transform. Relinquish responsibility, play the blame game, and everything will continue in the same vein. Ultimately becoming more and more unbearable and creating more pain and suffering. This is the victim identity playing out. The interesting thing about the victim is that it has to perpetuate itself to remain in our psyche. It is designed to kill us. The ultimate in victim consciousness is, "see now I am dying because of you."

Judgements are interesting lenses, imposed upon pure awareness, which have the dual results of creating limitations and restrictions for ourselves and the other being or thing that we superimpose our judgement upon. They create a freeze frame and the illusion of solidified energy, densely fixed, into a form. Judgements are like glue, they keep us stuck and disconnected from who or what we really are. They act to create perceptual viewpoints, distorting or enhancing whatever it is that we place our attention on. A judgement, be it constructive or destructive, is still glue and a holding agent. They are a fundamental part of the mechanics of desire and resistance, and both of these can generate or arise from, attachment. It is this that continues one part of the cycle of pain and suffering. Judgements and discrimination are part of the fear matrix, stemming from ignorance, low self-esteem and arrogance.

To free ourselves little by little from the affects of judgements, the play of desire and resistance and attachment, is to give ourselves a gift of freedom, of space, of peace, of trusting and of allowing. It is once again taking a step out of the matrix of fear and into the matrix of love. In turn this creates even greater space, freedom, peace, trust and allowing for others and all things in our lives, to be just as they be. This is indeed an expression of love.

I had done many exercises exploring the effects of judgements and with the concepts of desire and resistance, but one of the most awakening experiences occurred within my family. I watched myself in the situation as both an observer and as a participant. I was fully in the experience, yet unwilling or able to stop it in its tracks. It was as if I was to be witness to it, whilst simultaneously experiencing it, in order that I get the full impact and experiential clarity of its lesson.

I had chosen a less conventional route in my family, after many years of fitting into the conventional. We, two siblings, one older, one younger and I, had chosen our professions all of which were socially acceptable. I had started out as a teacher, yet after eighteen years I had become disenchanted with it. I decided to go out on a limb and pursue the spirit calling to go into the healing and liberating arts field. At this stage I was a reiki practitioner and a personal coach. I was also facilitating a liberating arts programme, enjoying my artistic inclinations.

I was living without a regular income and with no savings to cushion any dry patches.

I agreed to meet my younger sibling and my parent in a third country and put off a week's work in order to show up for the family gathering. I felt I should be there, though, if the truth be known, I did not want to be there, I wanted and needed to be doing the work. This was all part of the pattern of not being good enough, a display of the disease to please. See Harriet B.Braiker's book *The Disease to Please,* and my actions were a blatant self-betrayal and self sabotage. I couldn't see it at the time however. All I could see was this was something I had to show up for and I used it to add more substantial evidence to the belief, *my family always want something from me.* Clearly even that was back to front, it was me wanting something from my family, their approval no less.

Already feeling stretched from the airfare and on edge, walking through the city of commerce and endless shopping malls filled with shoppers, I made my way to the apartment, chattering in my head about how *they would judge me because I didn't have any money, well at least I didn't have as much as they had, because I didn't have a real job, because I was a failure, because, because, because.* A thirty minute walk where I annihilated myself and contorted into the most contracted, defensive form I could get into. By the time I reached the apartment I could not even look at my family, let alone speak to them in a welcoming way. My barriers were up and the weapons were drawn, and they had done nothing.

The day unfolded and although civil, things did not improve. Later that evening, while conversing with a third party and looking for solace, the story began to unravel. As I talked I started to see and tears began to flow. I realised that actually regardless of how, whether or if, my family judged me, it was my reaction to the judgements, that were a clear signal that actually those judgements were all my own, about myself. I had disowned the judgements, making everyone else unkind, unfair and mean and was feeding my victim identity to the nth degree.

As the tears fell and my heart cracked, it opened a little wider. Movement from within was occurring, and this meant the seeds of transformation would now have more space and potential to grow. I decided to look at all the judgements I thought others, in this case my immediate family, had on me and I owned each one as my own. This generated the elements of compassion, forgiveness and acceptance. Firstly, directed from myself to myself and then from myself to my immediate family.

I did the work internally that night and in doing so created a completely different environment the next day. It no longer mattered what judgements others had of me, once I had handled my own part. Their judgements were whatever they were and fear of them no longer held me stuck. This also meant that my perception of them began to change over time. A layer of the victim identity also fell away that evening.

A clear signal to look within comes when we feel that the external world is coming at us. Clearly it is not and the sooner we allow ourselves to embrace that, the more harmonious existence becomes. Other examples of such plays of judgement are experienced by all of us everyday, regarding people, places, things, feelings and so forth. As we become more familiar with our own self-deception, we begin to realise that anything that irritates us about others, is a signal to look within and know ourselves better.

A person walking down the street in different clothing and with a different appearance from most others in the street, may elicit all sorts of different responses, peppered with judgements. For example; intimidating, interesting, odd, threatening, gentle, tough and so forth. In addition maybe the thought, "oh please don't stop and talk to me," the resistance, or the desire "oh please do stop and talk to me." The mechanics of fear are that we attract that which we fear.

Whatever we perceive the being as, is exactly what we will experience. Judgements act as lenses through which we filter our experience. Resistance tends to draw something to us, while desire tends to push something further away from us. Both require attention and energy to perpetuate them, and neither allow us, to experience what is, just as it is.

Try meeting an old friend, without any of the beliefs and judgements you have about them, in the way. Stay open to meeting them exactly as they be, right there and then, in that moment, and be willing to be amazed at the refreshing experience which unfolds.

What are we doing when we judge something to be this or that, good or bad, right or wrong? We are operating from a state of duality, of disconnect and we are separating ourselves from All That Is. We are blocking the energetic flow of what is, and we have taken ourselves out of the present moment and created yet more illusory stories. We move in and out of proximity with the object, be it of a person, thing or feeling, making it personal by identifying ourselves with it and then in turn making it impersonal, less cared for, distant and outside of ourselves.

Feel each of the following statements and picture where you are in relation to each one?

My child - your child - their child - child
My life - your life - their life - life
My phone - your phone - their phone - phone
This child - that child - good child - bad child - child
This life - that life - good life - bad life - life
This phone - that phone - good phone - bad phone - phone
Right child - wrong child - child
Right life - wrong life - life
Right phone - wrong phone - phone

With emotions it is the same. Happy is constantly seen to be something to aspire to. It's a good emotion. Sad is to be avoided it's a bad emotion, patience versus anger, clean versus dirty and so on. It is our judgements that continue to create both sides of the dynamic, seemingly in conflict with each other. Whatever one resists, persists. These very judgements then trigger the desire or resistance within us that then compounds the existence and presence of the object. The more we fight something, the more it is there. The more we desire and crave something, the further away it seems to be. The more we can have of it, the less we feel we have. Our attention is on what we do or do not want, because of the superimposed judgement we have placed upon it. That judgement may or may not be compounded or generated by society. The effect it has on us is that we are no longer right here, right now, experiencing what is and what we are.

I love this or that feeling creates a patterning of desire and of grasping. *I want more and when I get it I'll do whatever I can to keep it.* This is coming from the matrix of fear and its friend and ally lack. *I'm afraid it will go, I'll never get it back, I'd better keep it, someone else will want it, I don't have enough or I won't have enough so I won't share it. I'll keep it and protect it and hold on to it.*

And then we are no longer even experiencing the "it" that we so love, for all the attention has moved on to how to keep it, get it again and protect it. This separates us further from our fellow beings and from the cycle and experience of life.

Just like the breath, which comes into the body and goes out of the body in its own natural rhythm, and in the same way everything else comes in and out of our lives, following its own rhythm. The fixing of it takes us out of this natural rhythm, and propels us straight into the oscillating duality of illusory life, in which we struggle to survive, moving between one polarity and the next. This is not life. This is our own story and it is coming from us, therefore it can be changed. Simply, gently and gradually, by dropping the judgements we all too readily impose upon and project out into the world.

To start right where you are today is the key. No need to churn up the dirt and dig deep into the past. That will show up when and if required. To meet ourselves where we are right now, to catch the judgements that are creating the life we are experiencing in the present, is the first step to consciously and deliberately making the space to allow who we really are, to begin to emerge. We can raise our own level of awareness, observe more of what we create, of what we see and of what is our reality.

Here is an effective technique:

Make a list of your closest ones, family, friends and colleagues.

Write down how you think they judge you.

Sit with each one and this is the key, take each one, one by one, until you are able to fully feel how it is to embody that judgement.

Own each one as your own judgement about yourself.

Accept each one as your own judgement about yourself.

Forgive yourself and forgive the others. Stop holding the judgement against yourself and allow it to dissolve.

Judgements occur on a more global level as well. We are conditioned to function in a society and world where judgements predominate. Opinions are generated in order to generate commerce. Marketing is a very powerful tool. Opinions or judgements play into the psyche of core beliefs, especially those of not being enough.

Advertising has one purpose. That is, to sell us a product which we do not need, nor had we ever thought of needing prior to the campaign. Social divisions are created neatly and effectively, without most customers being consciously aware of the manipulation that is occurring to their psyche, or to the detriment of their fellow beings on the planet.

Advertisments are designed so that we can have the same as everyone else, be the same as everyone else and ultimately, be as good as, or better than everyone else. This desire is resulting in a disparity and a gap that widens and widens. Judgements, resistance and desire, all feed into this illusory life we become immersed in. It takes will-power to stop and have a look at it, as it really is.

The environment is presently and predominantly abused to an extreme extent, to fulfil these false desires. Rare earth minerals which are used in so much of the latest technology are relatively harmless when they are in the earth. To extract them from the earth however, creates highly radioactive soil. Tons and tons of soil is processed to produce very little of the minerals. This is driven by judgements which are fueling our desire to have the latest thing, and be better than someone else. This is driven by advertising campaigns, which is driven by the desire to be the number one producer, which is driven by the fear of losing the top position in the market, which is all driven by the matrix of fear.

There is no one root cause, as all things are interconnected and interdependent, yet if we look at nature and we look at our desire to control nature and the effect it has, we can actually see how destabilizing that is. Amazing that we judge how nature shows up. We judge everything.

We can look at how our presence and our desires are contributing to environmental disasters in the making. We can try to assess if they are actually our desires or simply something made up by external market forces. We could start coming up with and instigating our own alternatives. Then individually and collectively, with awareness, we can and need to start to make changes.

We can be more aware of how we may be allowing ourselves to be ensnared and step back to address that identity, belief or judgement, so that we can move freely in our lives and have things move freely into and out of our lives, in harmony and balance. We can move towards circulation of goods instead of accumulation. The following websites share interesting viewpoints and techniques to make that shift *www.theminimalists.com* and *www.zenhabits.net*

There is no right, no wrong, no good, no bad, no this, no that. It is our attachment and our grasping onto it all that perpetuates the cycle of pain and suffering we find ourselves in. Only we can find our way out. Dissolving the judgements and the play of resistance and desire is key to doing this. It requires courage and a deepening of personal integrity to catch how, where and why we deceive ourselves so easily and quickly. It is this that will set us and others free to be.

Our lives are filled with opportunities to clean up, clear out and get real. The only things standing in our way are the beliefs we are operating through, the judgements we hold and the lies we tell ourselves.

Eight

Test or Opportunity - Integrity and Self-Deception

High up on a sea cliff, overlooking a pristine beach, the sun was setting and the session I had been receiving was ending. The therapist whispered "it's time to come back now." And then it hit me, as I heard my inner voice say, "It's too hard down there. I don't want to come back."

I was operating through the belief that *life is hard*. In that instant, my heart ached and I returned to the present. That was the first time I bumped into that belief with such clarity and certainty, and it took a few more fortuitous occasions to fully accept it, own it and let it go.

I, like many others, friends, clients and strangers, would say *"It's a test. Life keeps throwing tests my way. This is a test. I know it's just a test. Will I pass the test? What happens if I don't get through the test? What if I turn around and simply walk away from the test? Does it mean I'll be free and I can just get back on with the rest of my life? Or does it mean that it will show up in a different shape and form, in another area at another point in my life, perhaps bigger and harder and more intensely than before?"*

What is the best way to handle these tests?

It may be helpful to replace the word test with opportunity.

The most important thing to remember is that life is. Everything else is what we decide to impose upon it. We are creative beings and although we may not be consciously aware of it, we are creating all the time. Life is.

We decide if it's a test or an opportunity. Whatever events, circumstances, situations and people show up in our lives, how we decide to view them and respond to them, affects our experience of them, and on some level affects them too. If life being a test is helpful then by all means work with that. If however, it compounds the game of failure and success, and thus the mass consciousness belief of not being good enough, then I would recommend deleting the concept "it's a test" from all mental flies as rapidly as possible. Use the "spot it, stop it, drop it" process.

There are things that happen in life that require additional mental, emotional, spiritual and at times physical endurance. They are occurring as we have desired or resisted them at some level of consciousness, at some point in time. *"If you have been brought to it, you will be brought through it,"* is something someone once said to me, and so far it has been true.

It may mean that a way of "getting through it" is to walk away. For example, from an abusive relationship, from work which we are no longer in alignment with, from a country which stunts our growth or from a family or a friendship which undermines our very beingness. Whatever it is, there are indeed times when the way through a situation is to turn and walk away, with gratitude if we can. I see all of these as opportunities for dropping our self-deception and stepping up our levels of personal responsibility and personal integrity.

To walk away with gratitude is an act of love. Grateful for the lessons we have received and for the gifts that have been present, even if we cannot see them all, right at that moment. To accept with gratitude, the opportunity that is being given to us to step into what is in fact "right action" for us is an act of love we give to ourselves and to the other.

If we have been in an abusive relationship, be it personally or professionally and we are free to separate, our staying in that relationship and continuing to allow the other to abuse us is when we then become the abuser. We are at some level allowing or condoning their behaviour. We are making the other an abuser, which means we are in fact the abuser and they are being abused.

It is an ideal opportunity to look at how being a victim serves us, and then, seeing how the victim's flip side is the abuser. Both are within us.

This is the case for those situations where it is possible for us to walk away. I am not referring to imprisonment or child abuse. In these situations, talk to people, seek help. Ask others to help you, if you can. The above action refers to the day to day interactions we have with each other, which we tolerate, yet which serve neither ourselves, the other, humanity nor the community as a whole.

They are all opportunities for us to get real, to step up our personal integrity and to take personal responsibility. Responsibility, when defined in an empowering way, means: *the ability to respond to a given situation to the best of our ability at that given moment in time.* When we are out of integrity with ourselves it will impact upon every area of our lives, such as, in relationships and in business, and it shows up as sabotage and disappointment.

I experienced and learnt many lessons from my place of work. I worked as a teacher for eighteen years and by the time I was on year fourteen, I was done. However, I moved islands and continued to work for the same organisation. Initially working part-time and being in a new location suited me perfectly. I was paid by the hour, I came in and did my work and left. I worked three months on and had three months off.

The three months off were for me to work on my own art projects, and to live life without having to be anywhere. The balance was great, initially. Then little by little, a few years later, the hours became more and the time on longer, yet hourly rates remained the same. The institution changed from a close-knit community, to a larger more commercial outfit. Along with that expansion, came a contraction in personnel relations. Suddenly the core of the product, the students, teachers and support staff, were no longer thanked for their contributions. Indeed they were often the last to be acknowledged.

Commerce can result in a forgetting of the human being, so focused and driven does it become by market forces and income profit/loss figures. Gratitude is an integral and essential element to business and every aspect of life. A part of me was dying in this new environment. The heart had gone out of the school and I found my motivation and energy went out along with it.

To continue on in anything, which we no longer enjoy, which we feel criticism and negative responses towards, which we are at pains to run down at any given opportunity to anyone who may listen in and outside the work place, is an abuse of our employer and the other employees. Our actions may justify why we wish to leave, or even make it easier for us to leave, but unless we actually take our grievances to the person who is best able to address them, we are acting with little or no integrity towards the contract we have signed. In turn, our ethics are equally questionable, even more so if we continue to stay on and work for the company. It is out of integrity to receive a salary and to bitch at the same time, without taking action. We are the ones who lose.

I did all of that for quite some time. Then I woke up one day and began to shift my perspective. Rather than complaining and projecting a blaming attitude, I decided to look at it as an opportunity. I woke up as I was seeing the same pattern come up when I was spending time with friends. I was forever complaining about the island where I had been living for eight years. I pressed pause and allowed personal integrity to come into play by asking myself the question, "What is really going on here for me?" Then I realised, I believed I needed to make it bad so it would be easier to leave.

If we have expressed our views to the departments concerned and continue to feel dissatisfied, then it is a clear sign that it is time for us to move on, even if we do not have a clear idea of what that may be to. That is what I decided to do.

Life at work may well have become dissatisfying because *we* are the one who needs to move. Especially if the dissatisfaction remains after the changes we desired have been addressed. It is not the company but us that need to shift, and this is a gift. Making something bad so it's easier to leave is a lie. When we're ready to go, we go. It is our story.

Fear keeps us in a holding position. Be it fear of not having other work, savings and so forth. Stepping into trust from this place is a challenge. Not stepping into it is poisoning our entire system. It is only in taking the step that we can open the way to the new. I know it is a big call. It is for each one of us to begin to generate trust, one step at a time. I did and do and it comes with challenges and gifts every step of the way.

This is where the art of gratitude comes in.

To take leave of a place of work, or a relationship, or a country with gratitude, respect and grace, is a gift to our selves, to our colleagues, our employers, our partners and to the nation. It will affect how we begin our future relationships with colleagues, employers, partners and countries. When we have difficulty doing this, it is helpful to move into a moment of reflection and recall all the things we have learnt from that time period. We may have learnt what we don't like, what we don't want and what we wouldn't do. This is still a huge gift. At least now we know.

In terms of the work place, we received a salary while we were finding out, which enabled us to live to some degree and to do some of the things we may have wanted to do, buying some of the things we may have wanted to buy. We can be grateful for this. We can reflect on the different people we've met and the opportunities that we have had to learn from others, to share with others and to realise and recognize through others. Even if some of them were mixed, we can be grateful for they are gifts none the less.

Look at the skills set we are going to be taking with us, which we didn't have before, even if it is standing up and saying "this no longer works for me". It is a skill to recognize and then to act upon what is right for us, and this place of employment has given us all of those things and paid us in the process.

Gratitude allows the heart to soften, which allows other doors to open with greater ease. We will be approaching the new as an adventurer and an explorer, not as a victim and abuser. There is a big energetic difference, and future colleagues and employers feel it. You feel it. Be what is going to serve you and everyone else the best.

Friendships and family relationships appear to be much more challenging. This is because they are usually so much closer to us, and the possibility that we may end up alone, feels much more likely, triggering fear. This as we now know, keeps us and the other in a holding position and that takes everyone into the continual cycle of pain and suffering. This is not about doing whatever we can do to change our friend or family. No, this is about us and our personal change or transformation. It is for us to do the work, for us to step up in being true to ourselves in a non abusive way. This is not about finger pointing, blaming and shaming. It's about us getting in tune with what is right for us, about us taking a good long look at ourselves. We are about to see how we deceive ourselves, loudly and clearly and that can be a little uncomfortable at first.

Our friends may do things we do not like, value or feel is ethical. The first thing to do with any criticism we have directed towards another, especially one that carries emotional charge, is to recognise it as a signal to look within. Somewhere, somehow we will be running the same thing, perhaps in a different shape or form, but for sure it's running somewhere.

For example, *people are unfaithful*, pause for a moment and reflect on how and where you may also be unfaithful, if not to others, to yourself. There are times we doubt ourselves before we go into a meeting, or times we would really rather stay in and read a book but go out because all our friends are going out, or times when we want to have a clean night but take some drugs because everyone else is. All these are ways that we are unfaithful to ourselves.

Any criticism, with emotional charge that we have about another being is a sign of self deception. When we point a finger out at another, if we look at our hand we will see an interesting thing, the other fingers are pointing right back at us. We are deceiving ourselves into believing that the world is coming at us. It is not. It is coming from us. Everyone and everything can be a mirror.

So initially to address a friendship or family relationship that pushes our buttons, we need to seize the opportunity and look within. Look at where we do the same, look at why we do the same, and look at what we are really feeling when we do it. I was very good at quick responses and expressed a rapier like wit. I could cut someone off at the knees within seconds and turn around and walk away, not giving my actions or the others' demise and feelings a second thought.

This had gone on for years and was in place to disarm and undermine others, so I could feel powerful within myself, righteous and invincible. To fight with words, to deflate another and ultimately to inflict wounds upon others is encouraged in some circles. Debating societies, politicians, lawyers and barristers, are all clever at manipulating other's words, to trip them up, to run rings around them and to say "see you are wrong."

In other circles such skill is directed and tempered into innovation and transformation. In the former case a battle is won and wounds are inflicted. In the latter no battles are fought, no wounds are inflicted and the result is a synergetic agreement or solution, which is right for all, at the cost of none.

To look within, and see the underlying motivations for our behaviour, requires courage and a willingness to be vulnerable and open to what we may find. Vulnerability requires great courage and it is an action which will take us somewhere other than where we have been. It is key to freedom and discovering for ourselves who we really be. It allows us to own and acknowledge where and how we have operated from fear and inflicted pain upon ourselves and others, out of denial of what we were really feeling.

It creates the space we need to reconnect with our eternal centre in a place where we trust ourselves, our fellow beings and our environment. Vulnerability allows us to drop out of the mind chatter, out of the head and fall straight into the heart and the feeling centre in the belly. It enables us to be at peace and to operate from the matrix of love in our interactions with everything and everyone, to an ever increasing degree.

As I started to do work on the inner realms, noticing where I was criticising others for being negative or critical, I owned where I did it too and gradually started to drop that kind of behaviour from my own interactions. Remember you can only address your own side. I asked myself why I treated people critically and realised it was a reflection of my own unworthiness. It came from a lack of self acceptance, forgiveness and compassion towards myself. My fear of not being enough, meant I was keen to show how others weren't good enough, masking, denying and hiding my own shadows, through exposing the shadows of others.

And below that fear of *not being enough*, was *not being loved* and all tangled up with it, was *not fitting in, not being right* and *being wrong*. As I looked at each piece and owned my own feelings of inadequacy, I became more accepting of myself. I became more forgiving towards myself and the pain I had inflicted on others. I became more compassionate with myself, appreciating what I now knew and how I could now be.

This gradually led to greater acceptance, forgiveness and compassion towards others too. As I no longer needed to assert myself, by being dominating or crushing towards others, that identity and the behaviours associated with it, could just perhaps begin to transform into something more compassionate, more loving.

As the cutting wit diminished and the identity transformed, I stopped interacting in a defensive and cutting way. I was able to address the people in my life in a non accusatory way and in a way that was clear and free of emotional charge.

Just like a singles game of tennis, when one person stops playing, there is no longer a game. It is up to us to stop playing the game and I did so by stating that I would prefer to stop interacting like that. The other player, will either, go and find a new partner, or they will also stop playing. Whatever they choose to do is up to them. We are simply concerned with cleaning up our own field. It may or may not have a knock on effect to others, we may or may not be an inspiration, a pioneer, or a game changer. That is irrelevant or a bonus depending on how we look at it. Our embodiment of our realization is the key to life transforming on a deep level.

Everyone in our lives is a gift. They are all giving us the opportunity to meet more of ourselves and to be more of ourselves. If that is, we are willing to step out of the fear of losing them and being alone. I do not deny that there are times when taking this course of action results in exactly that, or so it seems at the time.

My life transformed fairly radically from being a social butterfly and party girl with a rapier like wit, to being a work in progress and one who is still on the way to becoming as authentic as she can be. Right now, I would like to think that I am a more open, authentic, softer and stronger being. I may be a little less confused, yet with flaws and an ongoing process, just like everyone else.

Initially it was disorientating, disturbing and downright uncomfortable, for myself and others. There were those who felt that I was judging them, through my decision to no longer play the games. The funny thing was, that it was the first time I could remember doing something that was actually all about me and not about anyone else, their expectations, their assumptions or their needs.

Some acquaintances became friends and some friends, like other acquaintances, found new people and we drifted apart. There were times of loneliness, which became times of aloneness, which in turn became times of gifted solitude. In between there were meaningful and at times frivolous interactions, with people who were more compatible with the being I was allowing myself to be. Some who seemed to have drifted away have returned, in ways that are increasingly genuine and supportive. All have been incredible gifts.

The best thing I did was to start being true to myself, no matter how frightening or seemingly painful that was going to be. To have stayed where I was, would have killed me, literally. I was trying to keep the peace and the status quo, for the sake of others from the fear of not being enough, the fear of not being loved and the fear of being alone. As it was, my spirit was dying a little more each day.

I had so disconnected from myself, in a bid to connect with others, that I stood no chance of ever really connecting with anyone deeply, for I was not there to actually do the connecting. I was being everything I thought or believed others wanted me to be, which meant I was out of the picture. I was already living what I was afraid of, without even realising it.

It has taken a full renewal of every cell in my body, seven years according to biologists, plus a few more and no doubt many more to come, for me to connect to what just maybe "me." I now spend most of my life attempting to operate more consciously and deliberately from the matrix of love than the matrix of fear. I wouldn't change a minute of it, well... no because each step I have taken along the way, has brought me to where I be today, and I trust that where I am today is going to take me exactly where it is I am to be tomorrow. We are perfectly placed all the time.

Orland Bishop of The Shade Tree Foundation, who facilitates profoundly life changing and inspirational work with communities in LA, once shared the following with me in conversation. *"Every meaningful interaction we have with another, a familiar person or a stranger creates an opportunity for another part of ourselves to show up."* (Bishop 2005)

I feel that we are here to become fully integrated beings, so the more of us that shows up, the more of an integrated being we become. The more integrated we allow ourselves to be the more the world we create integrates, and then imagine how that may be.

Our commitment to being all that we can be on the inner and the outer realms is reason enough to be alive. It is our gift back to life and an expression of gratitude to All That Is, which in turn is all of this. Everything and Nothing, and simultaneously, Nothing and Everything.

Each opportunity we dive into, and each time we step through our self-deceptions into personal integrity, we die a little. Metaphorical deaths play a big part in this journey of life. We die to who we are in order to give birth to who we are becoming. Dying to ourselves is the fundamental principle of growth. Metaphorical deaths are in fact a preparation, a letting go and a relinquishing of attachment to what was once seemingly fixed. I will come back to physical death in another chapter, but right now I am reflecting on the deaths we experience in becoming *"consciousness aware of itself as existence."* (Adyashanti 2013)

As we move out of one way of being into another, one phase of work to another or one relationship to another, part of us dies. The identity and the associated behavioural patterns may die from the mode of operating, the company we keep, the clothes we wear, the food we eat, the drinks we drink, all the way down to the way we live and the beliefs we have held. It is a natural part of the process and the cycle of life.

Look at the caterpillar, which began as an egg, became a caterpillar and then becomes a chrysalis inside a cocoon. Then it eats its way out, which it must do alone otherwise it will die, and it transforms itself into the butterfly. Then it will mate, lay eggs and die and then the cycle begins all over again. Plants do the same, why do we consider ourselves to be different?

As soon as we are born we are dying. The embryo dies and the baby is born. The baby becomes the toddler, who becomes the infant, who becomes the little one, who becomes the pre teen, who becomes the teenager and so forth. Each transition represents a metaphorical death and birth. We are, or more accurately our consciousness, is constantly changing, literally and that means we are dying and being born constantly as well.

It may well have been that such transitions were once honoured, acknowledged and celebrated by all. This practice does continue in communities closely connected to nature, and they are frequently marked with celebration and a sharing of community knowledge and wisdom. Within communities disconnected from nature, such practice has almost died out.

The marking of metaphorical deaths are something fundamental to us all as beings, and fortunately the acknowledgement of them is gradually being revived in Men's and Women's groups around the world. To do this in a conscious and deliberate way alters our interaction with ourselves, with others and with life itself. It is an act of gratitude to reflect upon the old and what is going. It is a rite of passage to move towards that which is coming. It is a gift, to arrive at the birth of our new selves and others and to do it with grace.

When we find a belief that has been having a major impact on our lives, such as *I am not enough*, handling it in the same way, radically alters our energy field. It has taught us so much and when we are ready for that concept, the identities and the behaviours associated with it, to dissolve, gratitude is absolutely crucial. This is healing the graceful way.

When I actually let go of the sabotaging identity connected to abusing myself, I actually wept and grieved. Although part of me wanted to let it go, another felt a strong attachment and needed time to grieve, to recognise, acknowledge and honour the gifts it had given me, even if they were negatively charged. That identity had assisted me greatly during the time I wanted to avoid life. It had kept me in a delusionary place, which had served me during that phase of my life. Only then as gratitude was felt, was I able to watch it dissolve and be free to transform. I was sad to see it go, for it had been a friend for many years. Or maybe it is more appropriate to say a frenemy, a friend who is really a saboteur. Following that, I was able and ready to move towards that which was coming, with an openness and sense of celebration.

Exactly the same process applies to the ending of a relationship, be it a love affair, a friendship or a business partnership. When we experience divorce, a house move, retirement, changing schools or college, even a haircut, who we were before those experiences, no longer exists. Our identity has gone. It is dead and that creates a space for the essence of who we be, to show itself, without the filter of that identity. How wonderful to re-meet ourselves.

This conscious metaphorical death allows us to reclaim our energy from what was. We will need all of our energy for where we are going, Letting that which no longer serves us go with gratitude and grace, means we are able to allow that which is coming, to arise with gratitude and grace. We can then be present for ourselves, others and life, with more gratitude and grace.

This reverence for what was, what is and what shall be, is about living life as opposed to rushing through it without awareness. It is this that alters the fabric of that which we experience as life. It is fundamental to the human being part of our nature and beingness.

Every relationship, friendship, love affair, business partnership, every job, work place, project, death, birth, adventure, dream, animal, plant, fish, river, ocean, land, house, home, car, bike and so forth, every single one is worth the "creation of time" so that we can press pause. We pause to reflect, to review, to grieve, to honour, to acknowledge, to celebrate and to thank that which is going. As we move into gratitude, we can then to step towards that which is coming with grace.

These deaths can trigger grief and or nostalgia for those we've celebrated at one point in our lives. These sensations and states of being deserve our time, to honour and experience them with respect. The sitting with them, allows time for reflection, time for an assessment and evaluation of the self that was before. The creation of time, creates the space for gratitude for the gifts to arise. This leads to a more gentle, compassionate and graceful stepping into the new self and all it can now be.

In contrast, the rushing through, from one to the next, is a way to avoid feeling, to avoid honouring and to avoid paying respect where it is due. It comes from fear and takes one further away from grace and the state of being real for ourselves, for others and for the planet. It leaves us being carried along by the river of life, as disconnected pieces of flotsam and jetsam.

Given the option I'd enjoy the deaths, as much as, the births and savour the spaces in between, for the reflections are leading to the next connections. This requires trust.

Nine

Trust - The Process of Life

Trust in the process of life, easy to say, wonderful to do. The one who trusts is the one who is free. Trust in yourself and you shall see. Trust in your intuition and you will be guided to all that is right for you. Trust in the process of life and allow life to flow through you fully. Trust and your life shall open up in ways you may be unable to imagine. Trust and allow yourself to receive what has always been, yet you were too caught up to see. Trust and the unfolding of anything in life will take on a magical air. Trust and you will become enchanted once more with yourself, with others and with the world around you. Everything becomes more fluid and free. Delight walks by your side when you engage more fully with trust.

This came through when I was contemplating trust, and what follows in this chapter and the next, is part of my evolving relationship with trust. I have learnt that trust and trusting is an integral part of our make up. It's something we benefit from nurturing within ourselves, towards ourselves, and in relation with and towards others. Largely experiential I share my experiences to illustrate the importance of it in our lives.

I hear the all too familiar refrain *"yes but, I would but, I wish I could but..."* It is the "buts" that are the block, the speed bump on the road, the resistance to a changed way of being and the attachment to familiar if limited ground.

Whenever we talk about trust, the memory of betrayal enters the field. It is worth noting, that for any betrayal we experience, first we have betrayed ourselves somewhere along the way. How? Well usually by giving our power away, by not listening to and trusting our intuition. Trust is about allowing, so that triggers control in the field too. Trust is about a willingness to take personal responsibility for where, who and why we are the way we are, so that we can clear ourselves, from the self imposed and acquired limiting beliefs, and layers of non-acceptance.

Trust or the absence of trust, affects every area of our lives for better or worse and the effect it has is great. So significant is it in fact, that it is surprising that so little time is spent reflecting on what it means, what impact it has, how to foster it and how to nurture it. Trust is essential and even more so during the most challenging of situations. Each person's biggest challenge is huge for them, and all things are relative to the source being who is looking at them. *The Science of Trust* by John M. Gottman, is a rich book on the topic in relation to relationships.

Nature is a beautiful mirror once again. Domesticated animals dogs, cats, rabbits and such like, are reflections of the treatment they receive from human kind. An animal, that has been shown love and affection, is trusting of most humans. An animal, which has been abused, beaten, shouted out and roughly handled, will be extremely wary of human kind. In fact just like humans are with other humans. Animals, being highly attuned to their senses and sensitivity, are able to sense if someone means good or ill. Their inbuilt instinctive centre is activated and they respond accordingly. When people are in fear, animals sense it and are wary, for violent action can often arise from fear.

As beings we become distracted, even disconnected from our intuition, we doubt ourselves, and as we doubt ourselves and what we are sensing, we step into the absence of trusting what is right for us, allowing the viewpoints of others to direct our lives. We get caught up in the distractions, which take us further and further from ourselves. The absence of trust results in disempowering acts and a relinquishing of responsibility. There follows a cycle of projecting our mistrust of ourselves onto others. If we are wrong we will eventually make others wrong too, simply so as to feel better about ourselves.

I began to get some experiential clarity and insight into the mechanics of trust, when I decided to step off the roundabout of my life. I was no longer able to pretend I was drawn to the work I had enjoyed for the previous eighteen years.

There were aspects of the educational institution that no longer worked for me, that is true. We were no longer aligned, and as the school had grown, the focus had shifted from humanitarian to commercial. Numbers appeared to become more important than the people doing the work, from the cleaners up to the top. Gratitude and expressions of it disappeared from daily view.

This shift, from my perspective, coupled with the external environment, indicated that it was time to leave. That external environment, I would appreciate later, was also a reflection of where I had been and it was something I decided was not right for me. In fact commercialism at the expense of humanitarianism is too great a cost.

I had no idea what I was going to do after I finished teaching and I had no five year plan. I didn't even have a one year plan. All I knew when I handed in my notice was that it was over. It was time for me to stop doing what was no longer right for me. I had pushed it for two years already, knowing it was time for a change, but *fear* held me in place. To be precise it was the fear of not having the income that I was assured of at the school. The holding on to that security was in fact a betrayal of myself and my inner knowing.

I can see now that I made it harder for myself when I did leave, because I was so depleted, in terms of physical and creative energy, that it took months before I could begin to formulate some sort of a plan for the future. Even that was on a week by week, or month by month basis. I also operated through the belief that *life is hard,* so I naturally created situations to support that belief.

Finding the hardest way through, lurching forwards one step and falling backwards one step. That continued for quite some time. However the art of trusting from a space deep within, that it was no longer right for me to be doing this work, regardless of the security net, was to me an act of courage. So began my journey to recover my internal sense of trust.

I thought I had three months to work out what it was I was going to do, before my visa would expire. Then on the 26th of December 2004 the South East Asian tsunami occurred. I was in a car driving up to the central region of Bali to an Eco resort, when news came through that our friend was needed up in Aceh. By December 28th on our return to the coast, my call came in saying that my visa would be cancelled within two weeks. The agreement we had made had changed and along with it my rest and planning time evaporated.

It became clearer over the next few weeks, that it was time for me to step out of the known and into the unknown. There was no firm plan dropping in. I knew what I didn't want to do and had a sense of what I did want to do. I wanted to work with the healing arts and to honour my creative side. The concrete how to, was something of a mystery right then.

I moved to a new country in the region, blessed in having a beautiful place to stay while I worked out my next move. The country I had moved to, was as commercial as the country I had moved from, was spiritual. I moved from Bali to Singapore. The spirituality of the new country was commercialism and that meant shopping and money appeared to be the temple and the gods. I can now see the irony of leaving the school because it was too commercial and moving to a country that was the same.

It was an interesting place to be at the beginning of what I can only describe as a walkabout that lasted a good two years on the external level and many more on the inner realms. I am in no doubt that more continues to unfold every day.

It was this that introduced me more and more intensely to the workings of trust versus the absence of trust. It activated my consciousness to the matrix of love versus the matrix of fear. I attempted to do something new for myself in a country where I knew very few people, and although some tentative steps brought results, the diminished resources once more brought me back to the white board. It seemed I'd have to start teaching again.

The first time I went for an interview, I felt physically nauseous. My body was telling me *no*, and so I was open with the owner of the school and apologised that I couldn't do it. I was fortunate as the owner replied with a "Fine, let's talk about what you really want to do". As I talked I felt less nauseous. We parted with an offer for part time work should it come up and I accepted feeling free once more. The significance of this meeting was to play itself out a month later, when I experienced a profound sense of discombobulation in who I thought and felt myself to be. The higher self really does move in mysterious ways.

In the meantime I had gone to Cambodia and fallen in love with Siem Reap and Bayon temple, along with quite a few of the lesser known temples at the Angkor complex. Siem Reap reminded me of the feel of Bali, and I felt at home, quiet in the mind and at peace in the heart. Returning to the commercial city of Singapore had me determined to make a push for working with the healing arts. The thing was, I didn't really know well enough to trust that Singapore was not the place for me, and that I would therefore be creating further struggle by staying. I had met some good people, who were supportive and encouraging. My heart however, wasn't in Singapore, so the energy I was putting into my new venture was less than 100 per cent. It was more like 30 per cent looking back at it now.

On the inner realms, there was a whole different story unfolding. I had been on a silent retreat just before leaving Bali, and had had the insight that I had lived my whole life through fear. I had asserted my bravery in a denial of the fear. That was a big one, and I realised that the fear was something I had taken on before I was born. The unravelling of that fear continues. The mediation course had a primary focus of healing the body, and being physically healthy, I used it to explore the other aspect impacting on the body, that is to say the mind. I continued to do the practice every day in Singapore.

My resources were at an all time low, which meant fear was up on the screen big time. As I sat that morning, I realised that I did not know who I was anymore and tears came. I sat for a while, until it became unbearable, and then I got up and turned on the television, a usual panacea to a less aware state. The first words I heard in the soap opera were "but you don't understand I don't know who I am". I quickly changed channels, only somehow hit the same button and heard the same words again "I don't know who I am". No getting away from it that way, that was clear, so I got myself out of the flat, and went to nature and the botanical gardens.

Nature has always given me solace, a sense of being and a sense of place. I walked, breathed deeply and sat up on a little hill, glowing with the bright yellow flowers of the Golden Shower trees. Breathing in, just letting the colours calm me down, I asked for help from wherever. I asked for guidance. I asked for a sign, and then the phone rang. Things happen quickly when we finally let go of all the resistance. I surrendered to a higher aspect of consciousness and it was there, ready and waiting.

The call was to ask if I'd like to do a month of teaching, just a few hours each afternoon. It was the secretary of the principle of the school I'd been to, in what seemed so long ago. I accepted, knowing I needed to help myself get on track, so I could then do what I dreamt of doing. I trusted the opportunity I was being given to bring some structure into my life on the external level, so that I could support my internal process of transformation more gracefully.

This led to a return of functioning as a self with definition, yet the internal dissolving of all I had been defining myself as, continued on a subtle level. I decided to go back to my roots and flew to the UK at the start of the summer. I took up a teaching position at the Eckersley School, my favourite place to teach, and spent time with my mother in the countryside just outside Oxford. I caught up with friends. I touched the land and saw my father from time to time, who helped me to retrieve other parts of myself. It was an extraordinary time.

The unravelling continued over a period of five or so months. I let go of parts of myself that no longer served me. I also retrieved parts of myself that I had long ago forgotten or abandoned, in my desire to escape from who and what I was and am. There would be times when the tears would fall unexpectedly, and others when deep joyful laughter would rise up from my belly. I was at times going to pieces without falling apart and at others, falling apart without going to pieces. This is what it felt like as the old definitions, behavioural patterns, thoughts and identities shifted, dissolved and integrated back into the whole. The space that was being created was equally in flux, expansion, contraction, expansion, contraction, and then at some point, things came to a more peaceful and gentle semi equilibrium.

My mother was amazing, letting me stay and not knowing what was going on or what to do. Providing space was all I needed, and giving me that sense of something solid, was the best remedy I could have asked for.

It was fortunate that I had worked on my anger and frustrations before I returned to the UK. My parents had divorced in my late teens, and although as an adult I could understand the perspective and action of my mother. I, the teen, was blaming, angry and resentful. This part of me, had taken great pleasure in being able to get my mother to lose her control. Using a self-deceptions signals process from Resurfacing®, I had addressed this particular identity, and thus when I returned to the UK my relationship with my mother had changed one hundred and eighty degrees, all because I had changed my projecting identity and allowed it to diminish and dissolve. Stepping up one's own level of integrity changes the external world we experience.

I learnt so much those five and a half months back in the UK. I also made a trip to the USA having been inspired by a conference in Bali for world community peace in 2004. Rev Desmond Tutu had spoken at the conference, as did Arn Korn Pond from Cambodia, and a line up of International community activists. All shared their stories of how creating a space for dialogue, truly listening to others and sharing stories, enables change to occur and peace to come into the field. We can all make a difference.

I went to visit LA and was hosted by Aqueela Sherills. I had the opportunity to talk with Orland Bishop and listen to speakers from The Cutting Edge. They were all working in communities to encourage authentic dialogue and peaceful resolution of conflicts, creating the foundation and potential for a different future.

Here too, I learnt about my limits and boundaries. I learnt that the life I had already led was a gift and that I too may have something to offer others. I learnt so much about communication and clarity, and being open and honest with oneself and others, regardless of any shame that may arise. I began to learn the lesson of pretending to be something other than I was.

In America, a plan was made for the future, and I returned to the UK with a focus and intention for my next move, to Cambodia. Interestingly, it didn't arise from within but was a response to a suggestion made from the external world. At this point I was happy to believe that another would know what was right for me, better than I would know myself. In that wonderful synchronistic way, everything did eventually lead me back to myself.

A group of us had planned to meet in Cambodia, to run through ideas and test a retreat, we had discussed putting together to support others to find their own truth and direction. I see the irony in it now. Firstly, that with that divine principle as the aim, I let another's suggestion for relocating to Cambodia become my own, with little deep reflection and tuning in. I accepted it and then set about making it happen. Many things did indeed begin to align.

I went to Cambodia and even though the planned meeting was cancelled at the last minute, I decided well what the bleep I'll go anyway, and so continued my journey into the unknown and the emergence of a transforming self. I trusted that it had all happened for a reason and that this was still a good place for me to go, and that I could make it work. Funny how life is and where the mind takes us. The second irony, being what actually happened while I was there. I did indeed find my own truth and direction. It was a nine month long retreat, mainly one to one, with myself.

As I left the UK, my mother wished me well and told me to enjoy life. My father acknowledged that now I seemed to know what I was doing, and that I was making a difference. I felt I had my parents blessing so to speak, and I left at peace for the first time I could remember. I was no longer running away from my country of birth, and where I had spent the first eight years of my life. I felt that now I could come back happily anytime I chose to. I no longer needed to escape. It was a great feeling, and although I choose to live in warmer climates and different cultures, I recognize, honour and love elements of that land and its people too.

Koh Samui in Thailand was my first stop after the UK, and here I received training in how to teach reiki. I was already a reiki teacher, yet the pedagogue within me was keen to study with another master. I was also in search of the sun. It rained for ten days and I was only there for twelve. As soon as, I had completed my studies with the reiki master, my first student appeared within days. This was to become a pattern for a while. I realised that I was being given confirmation that I was on the right track with this and that I was being supported.

However, that didn't stop me from pursuing the idea of continuing to teach when I got to Cambodia. Teach in a school, formal classes that is, not reiki classes. Somehow the healing arts were still relegated to being a side job, and something I did while doing my other work. Interesting how I see-sawed from trusting to not trusting

Cambodia was to be another incredible teaching for me. It was a country that, through its own re birth, created an ideal environment for my own metaphorical deaths and birth. In Siem Reap I was the practitioner and the artist, and I was happy up there. I felt at peace and as if much was possible. I felt the desire to bring reiki to the land so perhaps, via schools and morning circles, children who wanted to, could be attuned. Then they could send healing to the earth to assist the land to heal, and in doing so support the healing of the country and the people as a whole. I still believe this is a valuable contribution and one we can all make.

For some wonderful left brained reason I decided that if I was to make the connections, I needed to make with NGOs, it was better for me to be in the capital Phnom Penh. I thought they would be able to help me get this plan off the ground. I had not been to Phnom Penh before and from the moment I arrived, along with two friends from the UK, I cried. I was in more unchartered territory. I cried and I cried, and this continued everyday for the next three months, long after my friends had left. I had walked away from possibilities and a like minded community in Siem Reap to what felt like a black hole, a deep well of unexpressed grief, pain and disembodied spirits. I quickly became aware that the tears were a collective processing of Khmer Rouge times.

I had a nice apartment to live in, I secured work at a school and I gradually felt my way around the city. I had my things in Bali and some others in Singapore, and here I was attempting to establish myself in Phnom Penh, no wonder I was a little scattered.

In that first week at the school, there was an evening function for the staff. We went out and I got talking to someone who worked for an NGO. Our talk turned to healing, as they asked what I did and I said I was a teacher. "No what do you really do?" was the reply. I laughed and told them I was a reiki teacher and gave them my card, thinking little of it. Even then the higher self was doing its best to keep me on track with that "what do you really do?"

After a month of teaching in an environment that was quite lacking in integrity, I decided it was time to allow the practitioner to be seen and put an ad in the paper. That same day, the first person I'd spoken to that night, a month previously, contacted me to ask for a session. They had not even seen the newspaper. I believe that my decision to open up to what I really do, set many other wheels in motion in the energetic universe we are part and parcel of. The invisible world has many doors of opportunities. Trust allows them to open.

Life started to change rapidly. Different contacts came in, new connections were made, and once again the teaching in school was getting in the way of what I really felt drawn to be doing. Fortunately, it was so uncomfortable to be working at the school, that after three months I resigned. The next lesson in trust was about to arrive. I was now reliant on the healing work to sustain me, pay the rent on the flat each month and fund my day to day living.

I had put together and run a workshop called *Liberating Arts*, which is a creative workshop for dropping out of the mind and into feel, from which healing can then begin to occur. I felt this would be an interesting tool to make use of in any healing process, and especially for a community which has suffered and continues to experience abuse.

I did some work, with the youth group that Arn Korn Pond was working with, and we were able to witness the shifts that occurred when a conscious new picture of the future was created. There is a freedom from the past that comes when it is finally seen, owned, accepted, forgiven, loved and let go of. His talk at the conference back in 2004 had really inspired me. He had been forced by the Khmer Rouge to play the flute in the killing fields over the mass graves. It was a gift to be able to work with him and the group of young musicians he was mentoring and sponsoring on his own land.

I also ran the same workshop for individuals in the city and some of the participants worked for NGOs. It was from this, that later an NGO decided they would like me to put forward a proposal. This NGO worked with street children and counsellors.

I put in the proposal, resigned from the school and then it was a question of be still and wait.

I did have work with another NGO which worked with sex workers and their counsellors. Along with the private practice, I was just able to hold the space. However, as the waiting went on, I grew fearful that the proposal wouldn't be accepted. As soon as I stepped into the fear, all the other business stopped. When I let go and trusted that I would have the funds to pay the rent, then everything freed up and appointments would come flooding in.

Over the course of a month this happened many times and each time I became more and more aware that it was my own fears that were blocking and stopping the flow of energy that was actually supportive of what I was doing. As soon as I tried to control, by thought or deed what might or should happen, the fear of what might or could happen if it didn't come in, would arise and I could feel the flow of life force energy shut down.

I started to observe it and play with it. Noticing that when I stepped away from the fears or put my attention on to other things, or when I surrendered it up to All That Is or allowed myself to tune in and feel that it was all going to be fine, it was, right there in that moment, just fine. Then I could actually feel this flow of life force energy start to move again.

A friend, Wayne, likened where I was, at that point on my journey, to walking across a bridge, knowing that the bridge was there, but it was in such a fog that I could not see even one step in front of me. I had to trust that the whole bridge was there and that there was a plank of wood for me to stand on. This I would only know once I had taken the step. That really was an exercise in trust.

Later back in Bali, I was to hear a meditation teacher refer to a similar state as karmic suicide. We are not ready. We are never going to be ready, until we take that step. As soon as we take that step we become ready. So stop waiting until you are ready, just take the step. Yes, that requires trust. The trust that, that next step on the bridge shrouded in fog will be there. This is what taking a leap of faith is all about. It is one of the most exhilarating and transforming things I've done and one I continue to do. I recommend it to anyone who has the desire to be themselves and move through life as authentically as they can be.

The proposal was accepted, the work was carried out and the aims were accomplished. More work came, as so often happens, and at the same time the realisation that the city of Phnom Penh and I, were not the greatest match, became even clearer. I knew where I did not wish to be, but I did not know where it was I actually wanted to be and where was right for me.

At this point in my unfolding transformation I was becoming more aware of the importance of being present where I actually was. I realised being in three countries, was not assisting my presence with myself, let alone my commitment to myself, my ideas, visions and projects or anyone else.

All I had left in the UK was one small box in my mother's loft and some winter clothes in a draw or two. I was scattered between north and south East Asia. For some reason I felt pushed to wrap everything up in Bali so that I could finally be where ever it was I was then drawn to be, even if that was eventually back to Bali. It was time to let go of the lease on the house, pass on my things, store the books and find a long stay home for my dog Peri.

I have heard it said that a great teacher will appear in the form that is going to be most effective for you to receive your lessons and evolve as a result. Peri has been this for me from the moment he was given to me at the end of 1998. It is sufficient to say at this point that energy does move in mysterious ways and animals have so much to teach us, if only we'd listen more.

It felt good to be freeing myself up, and after fourteen months away, I planned a trip back to Bali to clear the decks and set a new course. Little was I to know how that decision was to set in motion the next piece I was to learn, specifically about personal integrity and love, as well as, synchronicity, clairvoyance and trust. I thought I was going back to pack up the house on the external realm, I was in fact going to clean up the house on the inner realm.

My transformation was about to feel like it had only just begun, all over again. A deepening of trust in the unseen was about to occur.

In the centre of Phnom Penh is a Wat called Wat Phnom, and in the quadrants close to the Wat, fortune tellers used to be allowed to run their businesses, offering their services to whoever was in need. The elephant would do its rounds and the musicians would play from time to time. The fortune tellers have now been moved on, most likely the musicians too. As for the elephant, he was getting on even back then in 2006, so may well have moved on too.

Amongst the fortune tellers was a Vietnamese lady who when she read, did so in French and Khmer, so it was advisable to go with a translator. She was the favourite amongst the people I knew. The first reading she did for me seemed to be a case of wrong timing, as a big gust of wind came and blew away most of the cards. Providence or a sign I was not to be read that day. Still I respected her skills for she had assisted my friends and been pretty accurate for them.

So the night before I went to Bali I went for dinner with one of these friends, who had actually just visited the fortune teller and she shared some interesting news she had received. "A friend of yours in Indonesia has lost something, something important to them. I may be able to help find it. They are ok. Don't go out for dinner after 08:00p.m. you must leave the house before and be back before 10:30p.m."

The only person my friend knew connected to Indonesia was me, and there I was in Phnom Penh and had lost nothing. We thought it was the 2006 Yogyakarta earthquake and thought no more about it. Until that was, I got home later that evening before 10:30p.m. At around 11:00p.m. a message came through on my phone. It was from Nengah, my housekeeper in Bali, saying he was "so sorry he did not tell me before, but Peri had now been missing for three days. The guest in the house had not wanted me to know".

I instantly felt my lower three centres lock and shut down, and I recalled the words of the Vietnamese fortune teller. The next morning on the way to the airport I contacted my friend and asked her to please go back to the Vietnamese lady and ask her for help to find Peri, as soon as she had time from work. Meanwhile I boarded the plane with a feeling of growing emptiness. I contacted a reiki master friend in Kuala Lumpur (KL) and asked him to tune in and see what he could find out. I called my contacts in Bali and started to get the word out on the street, asking Nengah to let the *Banjar*, the village council, know so that people could keep their eyes open.

Peri is a Kintamani dog, a prized breed in Bali, known for its intelligence, loyalty and intimidating bark. They are a Balinese mountain dog. A cross between a Chao and a Balinese street dog, recently recognised as a pedigree breed in its own right across South East Asia. They have a delightful character and incredible affection for their owners. All Balinese dogs and cats talk and Peri was no different. They do sometimes go missing but if the word goes out early enough they will be returned, sometimes freely, sometimes for a fee. I was shocked and I admit, incredulous that three days in and the Banjar had not been informed, and so little action had been taken to look for Peri around the area.

Landing late in the evening I made a point to stop at the big Pule tree close to the airport. This is a sacred tree for the Balinese and this one is especially powerful! There is usually a priest to give you blessings as you leave the island and blessings on your return. After fourteen and a half months away, I knew I was going to be calling on all the Deities of the Island to help me to find Peri. I apologised for my long absence, asked permission to return, and then asked for their guidance and assistance.

By the time I reached a friend's house I was exhausted and yet raring to go. Fortunately I had a photograph and organised to go and visit a paranormal in Tabanan, one who was known for her ability to locate lost things, as well as, to cleanse spirits that may be bothering a person's life. We thought it was worth asking if she had any insights on Peri. It was a long shot but nothing to lose.

Arising early in the morning I made my way to the house and began to look in earnest, while the tenant slept on into the mid morning. This of course only annoyed me further, for it turned out that they had shut Peri out of the house for many hours, so he had gone wandering off. Then they had decided to withhold that information from me. The fact that they were now sleeping rather than looking, meant that the level of resentment and anger was rising, and in my story, their behaviour was outrageous. Clearly I was unable to quite own it as all mine.

The reiki master in KL came back with the information that Peri was safe, well looked after and in a location within 1km to 1.5km radius of the house. I just had to keep looking and I'd find him. This gave me hope and encouragement. I walked towards the beach, then headed left to the main street and stopped at the top of a pathway, called Gang Bisma, just next to where a group of drivers from the village gather and park their cars.

We talked a bit and I stood there for a while, not sure which way to go, then I turned and headed back up to meet Ibu Dewi, the paranormal in Tabanan to see what could be seen. She couldn't tell me much, but her assistant took his time and told me to "keep looking and talking to people and well, if it's meant to be you will find your dog." Practical advice and at least it gave me something to focus my attention on. In the next few hours I was sticking posters up around the nearby streets, and restraining my temper when I met the tenant, as she was moving out her final belongings.

I moved back in to start packing up my things, and the growing frustration and anger began to turn into rage. Early on the third morning, when I was taking an early morning walk along the beach, I had a conversation on the phone, with the ex-tenant and could no longer contain myself when they expressed their curiosity as to whether Peri had been found. I was like the sacred mountain Gunung Agung in 1963 and blew my top, until finally seething, I hung up and stormed off up the beach.

Gradually it dawned upon me that my actions had been extreme and unfair. This was in fact my own story, and I had better move into ownership of it if anything was going to change, and so that I could apologise in a genuine manner for my outburst. Compassion was needed in the field and the surest way to retrieve it and then exude it, was to clean up my part. I had the tools and it was now as important as any other course time to use them to their full potential effect.

I decided right there and then to do a Walk for Atonement on the situation. I started with owning that *I had been afraid of saying goodbye to Peri so I had created someone else to do it for me.* I paused, burst into tears and felt like throwing up and then I took my next step. *I was afraid I'd never see Peri again, so I created a situation where someone else did it for me.* More tears, more nausea and another step *I was afraid Peri would never forgive me for leaving him those fourteen months so I created a situation where I didn't get to see him.* More tears and another step. *I was afraid he'd die without me, I was afraid I'd die, I was afraid his heart would break and he'd never love me, I was afraid my heart would break and I'd never be loved.* Twelve steps later I arrived right in the space of primordial love. *I was afraid I'd never be loved because I had left a being I love and who loved me, so I got someone else to lose him so it didn't seem like it was me.* I paused here and the tears fell for a long time. As I walked back after contemplating spans of time, I sent blessings to the tenant, to Peri, to Nengah and to myself. At the end, feeling more peaceful in my heart, I let it all go and sat looking out across the ocean. A moment later a dog came and sat next to me, one I'd never seen before and I never saw again. It had golden eyes and sat looking at me and then out to sea. I was grateful for the company and for the sign.

I realised that whether I found Peri or not I needed to step off the island for a few days, so that I could come back with a different perspective, that of a Bali without Peri. Then I could complete my packing. I decided I would go to Lombok and stay with a friend on Gili Trawangan. I also heaved my heart into my mouth and called the ex-tenant to apologise for my fury and for putting them in such a position. I left them alone to address their own part, if they so wished. It was no longer my business. It was time to let go of hope, let go of fear and to surrender. I was creating space in which things could change, and I surrendered it up to a higher level of consciousness and took the next plane to Lombok. Three days to bathe my heart in the clear aqua marine ocean and to be still on the island with no traffic. At that time, mid 2006, Gili Trawangan or Gili T as it is known, was still a very peaceful and pristine place to be.

I had forgotten about the Vietnamese fortune teller, and on my last day on Gili T, the information arrived. "She must talk to many people around. The dog is close by. Be open in talking to people let them know and see how much she cares for her dog. A man will bring him back to her." So I returned to Bali thinking, *okay I've got one more week before going back to Cambodia so it's time to give it one last shot.* A kinesiologist also checked in for me and confirmed he was close by, and that even if I didn't find him this visit, not to worry because at some time in the future our paths would cross again. This would become very interesting a few years later.

I did as instructed and talked with my landlord and the neighbours in the village, allowing my heart to be seen, and asking for their help from that authentic heart space. Then I booked a massage and just before I went to it, Nengah and I had a huge argument. I refuted the fact that he had cared for the house while I was away or for Peri, and wow did the sparks fly. It was a major clearing of our emotions and our sense of abandonment. Both of us had been feeling rightfully aggrieved and that meant there was nowhere for us to go. In classic cinematic drama I flew off to the massage. Ninety minutes later calm and having finally let go, in the last outburst, of all hope, which is part of the matrix of fear, I had created the space for something else to occur.

Nineteen missed calls from my landlord and Nengah combined, and when I got through to the message it was "we think we have found Peri, you have to come and see". I raced home and my land lord, Pak Wayan, drove me down the road back to Gang Bisma where I'd been ten days before. He walked me right down to the house at the end and the family there greeted me, and told me to keep going through the garden, right to the back towards the temple.

I kept walking and as I came to the temple steps, I called "Peri" and saw a brown nose, white fur with golden flecks and two big brown eyes looking back at me. I walked gently forwards up the steps and then everything else melted away, as mutual recognition followed and our hearts burst open, with his woofs and yelps and howls and my tears. We were rolling around on the temple floor, a ball of fluffy fur and arms and legs flying. The word went down the garden and then back up the gang. "It's her dog, it's her dog, its Peri, it's her dog". Even writing it now brings tears and I have been fearful to write it down in case it is time for another leave taking, that of Peri making his transition and leaving me behind in this dimension.

After spending some time with the family they told me how Peri had jumped into their garden from a construction site behind, in a very distressed state. They had calmed him and taken care of him as their own, and he had been loving and gentle in return. The family had had Kintamanis before, so there was a mutual understanding of the love that passes between the animal and a human companion.

I was now faced with the decision of leaving Peri where he was or taking him home with me, knowing that I was leaving in a few more days and that his new foster mum, Barbara would be taking care of him. The family made the decision for me by saying "he's your dog, he belongs with you, take him home". We hugged and true to the fortune teller's words, a man, my landlord, brought Peri home to me.

Peri and I had a big talk and he knew, better than I did, that I would come back and that I had some more work to do before that would happen. It was with his blessing that I was to return to Cambodia to complete my walkabout.

Some years later, after I had returned to Bali, I rented a small studio, which I turned into a healing room, down Gang Bisma in that very same family complex. Each time I drove there, I'd look at the temple and think, this is so familiar, but I couldn't remember why. Then one day the penny dropped with a loud clang and I ran to the family and asked, "aren't you the ones who looked after the Kintamani dog?"

Slowly they also seemed to remember and together we stepped out of the fog, and recognised and honoured our connection. I also remembered the words of Frederique, the kinesiologist, and thought *wow she was so right!* Peri and I would have met again if we had not been reunited back in 2006.

I now know, with experiential clarity, that taking responsibility for my own part in a situation can radically alter the outcome, and in this way we do indeed create our own reality. There is so much more to life than meets the eye. There is so much more that occurs and unfolds in the energetic field, and on the inner realms that then affects what we experience as life.

The following became a mantra for me: Trust, Surrender, Receive, Believe. Trust, Surrender, Receive, Believe. The more we can do that, the more our trust in the process of life will grow and the more our lives will flow with grace, gentleness and ease.

The fortune teller has moved on and although I have looked for her each visit to Phnom Penh, it seems our connection is also complete, in this life time at least. My ex-tenant did me a great, if arduous service, as I was given the opportunity to clean up my own house, and get on track with my own integrity, my intentions, handling my fears and taking responsibility. Peri taught me so much about love. The fortune teller, the reiki master friend Chris, and kinesiologist Frederique, all showed me how much can be read and seen from different perspectives and trusting different senses. The Walk for Atonement is an incredible process and it created the space for things to change, and that was instrumental for me to be taken to Peri.

It is true that the greatest teachers will show up in whatever form is going to be the most effective to assist us on our path of evolution. Everyone had their part to play, and Peri was and continues to be one of the greatest teachers in my life. According to those who operate in those fields, he has been with me in every life time, so our connection stretches over our whole existence and for that I am truly grateful.

Peri stayed with Barbara and both were settled and happy before I left with the words "and if ever I come back to Bali I will be reclaiming Peri, everything else is yours to keep and do with as you wish." It took another eight months and then I was back to do just that.

Peri and I were reunited to our mutual joy in mid 2007. Not without another walkabout, on his side this time, just so he could make sure I got a great lesson in trusting my intuition and to deliver the message "it is time to come back to stay."

Ten

Trust - The Intuition

Intuition needs to be felt and trusting it, needs to be experienced. It is then possible to nuture it, so you can move with greater grace and ease along your spiral of life. I can only share with you my experience.

The experiential clarity that occurred through the events in Bali had a profound effect on me. My willingness to take personal responsibility for my part in the situation had created the space to radically alter the outcome. We create our own reality and the world is coming from us. It is vital for us to clean up from the inside out. That then creates the ripple effect, which has an impact on everyone and everything in our field and our circle of influence, and in turn, upon their circles of influence and so on ad infinitum.

I had experienced this realisation before, yet it was as a flash of insight. This time such a deep shift had occurred within me on the inner realms that I then watched it unfold in the external world and moved on. Many years later I consider that to be one of quite a few defining moments.

The person I had been underwent a major reconstruction and we're not talking cosmetic surgery here. I was no longer the person I had been before the event and it had propelled me onto a new trajectory of living and walking the talk of personal responsibility, in a way that would benefit myself and other beings from a more authentic and integral base.

I had seen and felt what happened when I had the courage and humility to admit my own side, and to consistently and deliberately step out of the matrix of fear and into the matrix of love. As I had allowed myself to be vulnerable, and show others what I was really feeling, the impossible became possible and the fixed reality became fluid and changeable, right in the now. I could not change the past action, yet I could and did change how I perceived it, and that allowed love to arise. It required self forgiveness and forgiveness of others, to create the space in which all things could change.

The internal shift had been so great that the next leg of my walkabout had a different feel to it. As I returned to Cambodia I landed with an "okay let's now get on with what I am here for". Finally I could be present with what I was there to do.

I lasted ten days in Phnom Penh, before the city and I felt totally out of sync, and I headed up to Batambang to a friend of a friend, who had a house with a garden and dogs. Normality gave me some respite, and gave my spirit time to integrate the inner shift in a more compassionate way than I had been doing in Phnom Penh.

Nature was and continues to be key. As Jean Liedloff, says in her valuable work with *The Continuum Concept*, it is in nature that one gets a sense of the "rightness" of one's place. (Liedoff 1977, 5) Everything falls into place in nature, for me, and a profound peace emerges from deep within in and permeates every cell, particle and atom of my being. I spent a week walking barefoot on the grass, touching the ground and exploring lesser-known temples taken over by nature. Then as my hair stopped falling out, my eyes became brighter and my step so much lighter, I took the boat down the Mekong River, back to Phnom Penh. What a gentle way to enter the city passing the water villages along the way and allowing the current to take with it the residue of the past few weeks.

To be ourselves, we are called to surrender to the current, as completely as possible. To become like a leaf in the stream, trusting fully in the wisdom of the current and allowing it to take us wherever we may be taken. Trusting it is exactly where we need to go and where we are meant to be.

The next few projects took me up to the provinces to run a personal development course for an NGO, who sponsored their employees to become more self empowered, present and personally responsible. On this course I was once again privileged to witness the power of consciously choosing to move out of the fear matrix and into the matrix of love.

The Walk for Atonement played a pivotal role. We were on day seven and the course runs for nine days. One of the participants received news that his young son was ill and had been taken to hospital. He immediately went into fear and his thoughts turned to the worst possible scenario of death and loss. After some coaching, he decided to do a walk on what could be worse than his son dying as result of his illness.

It was a big call and it took immense courage to do the walk and not run away from it, or create more fears around even doing it. The participant stayed on course after the walk, continuing with their programme. Within an hour the news came in that his son was out of danger and would be home that evening. We all breathed more easily. We had all witnessed the power of addressing what we fear, so that we could create the space for the possibility of a different reality to unfold.

Six months since packing up my place in Bali and placing Peri in dog foster care, I woke up one morning and felt the gentle tug of an invisible cord, coming not only from Peri, but from the island of Bali. In fact Peri was such an intrinsic part of Bali for me that it was one and the same thing. I didn't pay too much attention at first, wondering if it was just nostalgia and would pass.

I continued on with my business, enjoying the eclectic work I was doing and even secured a meeting with officials at UNESCO to discuss the dream I'd had for introducing reiki to young children in schools, so that in a morning meditation they could send love and healing to the land. The idea was surprisingly well-received, however, they had no funds to support that, let alone much else of artistic and creative value or of a holistic nature. An emerging economy is often hampered by a desire for all to have a piece of the proverbial pie, which leaves little funds for the actual work at a grass roots level.

Instead I continued to work with the sex workers, street children and their therapists, my private clients and prepare for a Time Out retreat for staff at NGOs in the development sector. As everything flowed I contacted my mother to let her know I felt to leave Cambodia. My time there was done and although I wasn't 100 per cent sure of the next move, I was sure that after nine months it was time to move on.

Nine months is the time it takes for an egg and sperm to meet, to become one, for a foetus to form and for a baby to be born. My gestation period was over and I was about to be born. As is so wonderful with life, I finished my stay in Cambodia coming full circle, with a master in residence at a hotel up in Siem Reap. It was the sister hotel to the one I had started at when I first arrived in Cambodia. The message was clear, even if I hadn't yet fully embodied or committed to it "focus on the healing arts, be that hands on or hands off healing, workshops and retreats."

I spent time at the temples in the Angkor Wat complex and then headed off to Vietnam, where I started to breathe more deeply. Then on to Laos, where I felt not only that I could breathe more easily but it was as if everything inside me could open up as well. The chakras or main energy centres expanded to take in the new.

Cambodia gave me a great gift and I return on a regular basis, to connect with old friends, make new ones and to connect with the land. I see it transforming and in some places, on some levels growing lighter. It too has been through such dramatic death and birth and is currently coming through adolescence into adulthood. In 2007 over 70 per cent of the population were below the age of twenty four. The Phoenix is rising from the ashes.

Not yet ready for a full return to Bali, I based myself once more in Singapore. There I agreed to go to Ethiopia, to share my experience of working on programmes for English for academic purposes, and to assist in setting up a course. I saw it as an opportunity to revisit the country that had started my life overseas at the age of eight, and which had had such a remarkable impact on me. Negotiations were long and laborious and I found myself fulfilling another dream before the trip down memory lane. Both were to teach me more about myself and more about trust.

Gross Domestic Happiness and the Himalayan Kingdom of Bhutan, was calling me and had been for many years. I had been to Nepal in 1994 and looked into the distance towards Tibet. I was standing five km away from it. The Kingdoms of Nepal, Bhutan, Sikkim and Tibet had drawn me ever since I could remember. The roof of the world was where I wished to be. When I was given the opportunity to go and spend some time there, my heart burst open with joy.

Once there I was in wonderment, for everything glittered and sparkled as far as I could see. My smile filled the valley of Paro and met the blue, blue sky. In the soil there was so much mica, that when the sun shone on it, it glittered and sparkled like the most enchanted land. As the sun went down, the mountains seemed to change to blue. I felt I had come home.

My younger brother was with me and although we had different viewpoints and responses to experiences, the Kingdom of Bhutan touched both of us in a wonderfully beautiful way. I am so grateful to have returned to a country that felt like home.

It was here that I was given an opportunity to integrate the lessons of listening to oneself, listening to the intuition and doing things because they are right for you and not for others. By listening, I really mean trusting myself and trusting my intuition. I was offered an extension to my stay in Bhutan, however it seemed that the project in Ethiopia was about to happen. To please my father and his Ethiopian connection, I turned down what felt so right to me, which was another week in Bhutan. I returned to Singapore, promising myself to return to the country and the people who had deeply touched my heart, as soon as I could.

Within a week I got the lesson, the trip to Ethiopia was delayed again and my desire or let's call it the disease to please, had well and truly slapped me in the face! There was more to come, and it seemed that that layer was up, as far as trust was concerned. It was about trusting my intuition, whereas before it felt like the lessons were about a more general level of trust. Trust the process of life and the art of allowing.

This time it was about trusting the internal guidance and to really tune into this, I realised that I needed to have no hidden agendas or ulterior motives for my actions. In addition to which, I needed to be still. It is impossible to listen, trust and act upon our intuition, if we are jumping about, fragmented and scattered all over the place. There is way too much interference and too many distractions in the field, for a clear sense of what is in alignment with our highest good to come through. I was clearly getting my lessons the way I needed them, and it seemed I had a hard head, because I was getting them in a pretty hard and fast way.

Intuition is the most incredible gift and is one which we all have. It's free and in my experience, it will only take us to a place we are meant to be. It is our own personal internal guidance system. Our own radar or GPS and if we were only to listen to it more, to operate from its input, in harmony with the heart, and then ask the logistics centre in the brain to get us wherever it is we are going, our lives would unfold in a surprising and magical way. *Intuition*, a book by Penny Pierce, is a worthwhile read.

We are however, encouraged and conditioned to disconnect from our senses, especially from our intuition, from a very early age. There has not been a very good press throughout history, for those who follow their inner knowingness. I mean, look at all the burnings and drownings, which occurred to so-called Witches and Wizards. The Harry Potter books and films may have gone some way to reinstate them and give children and adults an opportunity to focus on the acts of magic that happen when we trust our intuition.

As our lives become filled with external stimulation and distractions, it is little wonder that we do not hear or pay attention to what our intuition is telling us. Unless, that is, we find ourselves in a crisis situation. Although even then, rusty from disuse we may not trust the guidance we are receiving. Here's a technique we can use anywhere and anytime to connect to our intuition and develop our levels of self trust.

Whenever we are faced with a situation and making a decision, a phrase I have found useful to remember is *when in doubt, leave it out*. If however, we are sure we need to make a decision and we wish to make one that is in alignment with what is actually right for us, the following technique is most helpful.

With your attention on the situation and decision you are considering, connect to your belly brain, just below the belly button and see how it feels. This is where our gut feeling seems to show up. This centre monitors the environment so we can respond accordingly to what arises moment by moment. It will give us a reading on how comfortable we feel about the decision we are considering. I find placing the palm of my hand over the area makes for a deeper connection.

Next connect to your heart centre and see how it feels about the decision you are considering.

Then connect to your head centre and see how it feels about the decision you are considering.

Finally, taking all three feelings, come back to the heart centre and ask for the real answer to how you feel about the decision. Let the intuition, the inner knowingness arise. Once you have a sense of that answer, and both the belly brain and the heart centre are strongly in agreement, they can then let the head centre know what is right for them. It is then time to ask for the logistics in the brain to bring that decision into being.

It is only when we are moving with our three centres in harmony, that we are aligned to our authentic selves. All too often we are living in the head and disconnected from the wisdom of the heart and the belly brain. To develop the intuition further, take time each day to drop into the heart and the belly brain in all sorts of different situations. For example, when you meet new people, or make every day decisions. Discreetly, close your eyes, take a breath and ask each centre what it wants and then take all the answers back to the heart and ask for the real answer. Trust what you receive and act upon it.

The importance of tuning in to our own radar or GPS is crucial, if we are to become more present in our lives, transforming the way we operate in and experience life. The dropping of debilitating self-doubt and dissolving another tenticle of the fear matrix, occurs when we start to listen to and follow our intuition. For that to occur, other areas in our lives will also come under scrutiny, such as the identities and beliefs we employ to move through life. As with most things, one thing seems to lead to and impacts upon another. Start where you are right now, right here, and the rest will reveal itself as and when it needs to.

Not listening to and acting upon intuition, from my experience, involves self betrayal. We often prefer to see betrayal as coming from the external world first, until we look more deeply. Then we find it is our own betrayal that has brought us to where we stand at that moment.

Uncovering self-betrayal requires honesty and compassion, courage and the willingness to be vulnerable. It requires forgiveness and acceptance of self and of others. It brings such freedom, peace and excitement, that the humility and vulnerability required to integrate those self betrayals, becomes easier to allow, generate and hold.

The following occurred to me in late 2006 and I have been listening to my intuition ever since, with an ever more sensitive ear. The events changed my perspective, transformed aspects of my life and shook up my relationships. Interestingly both of them involved dogs.

It was December 2006 and a trip to Bali felt good. I just had time to catch up with friends, touch base and refresh, before going to Cambodia early 2007. There I was to facilitate a company retreat and then, if it came through, visit Ethiopia for the educational project.

I decided to spend the festive season down in Bali, and to do a little business, exploring the possibilities of being a Master in Residence, at resorts on the island. I knew it was time for me to spend some time with a friend I hadn't seen for eighteen months, yet when another friend called in tears, and asked me to stay and give her support; for her life and relationship were proving to be extremely challenging, I did not hold true to that which I knew to be right for me. I changed my plans.

I didn't have the awareness I now have to say no and listen to my intuition. Instead, I responded with a mental verbal yes, rather than from my heart and belly, which was saying, "No, this is not right for me". The mental yes was coming from a syndrome so well written about, by Harriet B. Braiker, Ph.D. in her book called *The Disease to Please*.

I felt I needed to validate my place on the planet, and to do that I needed to be needed. In fact, I wanted to be needed and that needing to be needed created a chapter that has taken quite a few years to unravel and integrate. Within its dramatic unfolding, have also come extraordinary gifts, which have brought me to where I am today. Traversing the spiral of life has been such a transformational experience. I am grateful for the lessons and the gifts of self trust and the intuition, even if I am still integrating them all.

Right then, my friend needed me and even though her two Rottweilers were not the friendliest of dogs, and had tried to nip me on the ankle before, and even though I had serious misgivings about them and the fact that they had bitten other people, I overrode all of that, because my friend needed me. Not once did

I reflect on what I needed, even on what my other friends needed, or on the fact that I could still see the troubled one even if I wasn't staying with her.

The initial days were fine. All went well. I saw friends and felt strong, high and empowered to be back in Bali. I set up a meeting with a resort to discuss a Master in Residence stay for 2007 and on Christmas Eve, I went over in the afternoon for the meeting. I would attend a dinner at my hostess's house later that evening.

The meeting went well. The dates were set and life couldn't have unfolded and aligned better. I would be there on my return to Bali. Then only ten minutes later, having left the resort facing a forty five minute drive back to dinner, I stopped at some traffic lights. I felt like I was watching a film with my eyes wide open, I saw myself walking into the garden and being attacked by the two Rottweilers.

I could not get the image out of my head. I decided to use every dis-create tool I had in my toolbox. Nothing appeared to shift it and strangely I kept right on driving towards the house, full speed ahead. I stopped to buy flowers and called the hostess on the phone; she didn't answer and after repeated calls there was still no answer. I arrived at the gate. Again, I called on the phone, I could hear it, but my hostess did not pickup. Eventually I shouted from the gate until she appeared and I asked her to lock up the dogs. The response, "don't worry, you'll be okay. I'm here." Once more I asked saying "you don't understand, please lock up the dogs." Again the same response, "You'll be fine, they know you, I'm here, its okay." I didn't bother to explain what I had seen, thinking perhaps I was crazy and that of course I would be okay, the owner was there. So I listened to someone other than myself. I opened the gate and began walking the 200 meters to the kitchen, where the hostess was standing.

A bunch of flowers in my left hand and a weighty full faced motorcycle helmet in the right hand, I walked in slowly. At about two meters from the house, the hostess turned to go inside and in that split second, the dogs leapt into action. One to the left ankle and one to the right lower thigh, just above the knee. I made no sound. My helmet smashed down hard on the dog on the right side and the flowers connected with the dog on the left side. Fortunately, they both released and at that moment the hostess, turning to witness what had happened, broke the silence with her screams. I still made no sound and the interesting thing was that I felt nothing. I had watched it happen from outside my body.

I left that house the next day and have returned only once, in all the years since, knowing that the dogs were safely locked up inside their kennel. I was not the only one to be bitten and I was not the last to be bitten either. That friendship fractured and although there was still contact, it transformed beyond all recognition from that which it once was, which was a good thing in many respects. The closeness however, was kept at arm's length for a long time and the new chapter within that relationship, continues to unfold. Seven years on, the time it takes for the cells to replace themselves, something new in the friendship is beginning to be revealed and it is a gift on every level.

The lessons or gifts that I received from that shocking experience were manifold, and I wonder now where I'd be without that having happened. I knew that somewhere, somehow, this had come from me. Well, at least the part that impacted upon me was coming from my own side. Whatever was impacting upon the others was whatever it was. The only piece I could address, at that point, was my own part in its creation. There was a lot of material that was clear, and it took me months and then a few more years to unravel it all, one step at a time. There were layers of beliefs, judgements and forgiveness to address.

The first piece that arose was that I had not listened to myself. I had not wanted to hear what I knew to be true and right for me. Not listening to my internal radar was huge. If I did not listen to it, why should anyone else listen to me? The belief that *I'm not heard* was what I experienced when the dogs decided to have a taste of me. Other beliefs such as *I do not hear myself, I do not listen to or trust what I hear from myself,* all came into view a few days and months later.

I didn't have so long to assess what had happened in the days following the event for I was getting ready to go to Cambodia. Then the second dog event occurred.

Now safely ensconced at the friend's house I had originally felt it was time for me to catch up with, I thought about offering to stay at Peri's foster mum's house, while she was away on a three day workshop. Then I cancelled that idea. The rational mind saying that would be unsettling for Peri, as he, the cat Matey and Barbara, the foster mum, had only recently moved to that house. I had sent reiki, with the intention that they stay close to their foster mum so that I would always be able to find them. I had shared that with Barbara so we were all on the same page.

So once more I decided to follow the rational mind, nurse my leg wounds and stay away from my own dog, Peri. A day or maybe two after this fleeting thought, I received a call from a very distressed foster mother. She had taken Peri to a friend's house so that he would be looked after during the workshop, and although he seemed most unhappy about being there, she had left him there. A short time after she had left, the caretakers opened the door. Peri had seized his chance and run straight out of the door and was now missing.

Incidentally, I got the lesson instantly. If only I'd listened to my intuition and offered to stay at her place with Peri and Matey, then the situation could have been avoided. Now clearly it was all to teach me to listen and act upon my intuition, and to stop ignoring the intuitive messages that I was receiving at that stage.

Once again results of the same belief showed up around not being heard. *I didn't listen to myself and therefore others didn't listen to my knowing or what I had told them.* Animals are such incredible teachers and they really do listen on the energetic level to what you tell them. Peri's actions were proof enough of that, as he aligned himself to the reiki energy I had sent. He was trying to find his foster mother, so that I could find him when I came to get him.

Incredibly, the search for Peri was on again. This time it was a shorter one and the miraculous happened in the most mysterious of ways. I called on all my psychic friends and they all said; "He is fine. He's with some other dogs, he'll find his way back and he's not distressed". I was sending healing and directions, as was Barbara and everyone else we knew. The posters went back up and we started walking the streets.

I wasn't so mobile due to the Rottweilers kisses, but that didn't stop me being out and about on the second day. No luck. And so my heart began to sink. That night, my friend told me a story of another dog lost in Spain, who showed up many, many months later, jumping into a car she was driving to the amazement of everyone. She said "don't worry if you don't find Peri now, you may well find him when you least expect to, but you will find him." I listened, I absorbed and I hopped up the stairs to bed.

I decided to have a chat with head quarters, HQ. I was feeling totally defeated and I surrendered to All That Is. HQ means I called on all the supreme beings, gods and goddesses, the spirit of Bali, the angels, my guides and spiritual masters, I called in the whole team and after crying in my defeat and venting in my helplessness "you'd better have something for me to do, as you have taken everything from me!" When I was finally spent with all the despair, I surrendered and said quietly, "so be it. If it is for Peri and I to be together once more, please place him somewhere that I can see him and he can see me." And with that I went to sleep, ready to get up early and meet Nengah, who had offered to help in the search.

Up at dawn, I headed for the beach, and no sooner was I hobbling across the sand, than a call came in from Nengah, saying he thought he'd spotted Peri way down the beach, the other end of where I was. Amazed I said okay, and on his insistence I got back on the bike, and headed to the beach far from where Peri had gone missing. Bizarre but true. When I got there I was directed to a hotel and skipped through the grounds after a white dog, which even from a distance didn't look like Peri. When we were face-to-face it so clearly wasn't Peri that I laughed and said "okay, now I'll go back to where I felt him to be." Nengah agreed that he would walk up the beach and we'd meet somewhere in the middle.

As I drove up the main street, I raised my eyes and said, "so what on earth am I doing down here when I'm meant to be at Oberoi?" With that, my head was turned to the left by an unseen hand and there was Peri walking happily along the street, two streets away from his foster mum's house.

The absolute surrender the night before had brought the miracle I been asking for, and the angels stepped in to help me retrieve him and get him home. There was no traffic as it was still early. I parked the bike and called to him. He looked at me and winked. Then he sauntered off ahead. I followed as fast as I could, until he turned into a construction site. I called and still he wanted to play, until the workers started to come up the lane. He turned and came towards me. I looked behind and saw the open gate and asked an incoming worker to please shut the gate. Beautifully, he raced right into my arms and I scooped him up before he raced right out of them again. Breathing in such a sigh of relief, and gratitude was expressed all around.

I headed back to my bike, where another angel in human form, had secured it on the pavement. They helped us into a taxi, which took us the two streets to Barbara's home. Relief and joy filled my body and once more there were such lessons to assimilate. I knew then, without any doubt that I'd be back and getting my own place, as soon as the last two overseas projects were complete. Then Peri would no longer need to go missing to give me the lessons and the gifts that came with them, as I'd be right there to receive them in person.

I went to Cambodia and after that Ethiopia where I retrieved the last pieces of my childhood self. Driving past a big building in Addis Abba, a shiver made me look at it more closely. I asked what it was and was told it was the French Lycée. No wonder!

That was where I had gone to school for almost a year from eight to nine and a half years old and had learnt everything in French. I can't say I was exactly happy there. I do remember skipping in the first day and crying in the subsequent days. I remember it being vast, but then I was pretty small. I went to the central market and loved all the familiar smells. I got to eat *jerra and wat*, unleavened bread and a hot, spicy chilli sauce. I reconnected with the energy of childhood and that in itself was freeing.

By March 2007, I was back in Bali. Almost two years to the day since I'd left and gone walkabout in fact. My re-entry was as the healer and artist, rather than as a language teacher and artist. I knew my time to examine and integrate the lessons from that December would come, and when it did I was ready to take a few more steps along the spiral of life and get to know myself better. The beliefs that I discovered in order to clear them, were gifts indeed

> *It's dangerous to shine too brightly.*
> *When you're in your power people will cut you down*
> *It's dangerous to be powerful.*
> *Others don't hear and trust my knowledge.*
> *I don't hear and trust what I know.*
> *It's not safe for me to be powerful and shine my light.*
> *It's not fair.*

The identities were victim, victim and more victim.

The gifts were profound and meant I could begin to dismantle the need to be needed, the disease to please, the sabotaging beliefs, the limitations and the identities. This in turn meant I could begin to show up just a little bit more.

I could trust what I was being told by my intuition and that my radar and GPS was in fine working order. It was life enhancing for me to trust it and vital that I started to do so. I started to draw some boundaries and set some limits for myself, as to what I could or couldn't do for others. I started to listen more closely and feel more sensitively into what was right for me. I owned my own part in the creations and stepped up my level of personal integrity. I believed in the power and effect of intention and energy work. I enjoyed a more enchanted and magical world and my life began to take on a new energy. I started to really appreciate that I may well have something of value to offer to others. Combining my world lessons and experiences from my walkabout, I put together a retreat called simply The Retreat and re-presented myself to the community, who had known a different being.

Then I moved to Ubud. It was time for Peri and I to be reunited and for the next cycle of teachings to begin. This was to be a journey into and of the heart. Now that trust was becoming an ever present and deepening part of my life, I was able to allow myself to venture into the realms of the heart, my own heart, or so it felt.

Eleven

Reclaiming the Heart

The heart is so much more than just a pump. My experience with craniosacral therapy has made this abundantly clear. In some cultures the mind is seen as being the heart. Others, who work with sacred geometry and crystals, believe that there is a chamber in the heart, which is where the creator resides, be that in the form of the tetra graviton or a crystalline tetrahedron. The heart has such a place in the lyrics and literature of love. It is either breaking into pieces or opening wide, shattering or bursting and every moment of every day we are alive, it is contracting and expanding, contracting and expanding. How often do we thank our heart for that continuous action?

The physical heart, the metaphysical heart centre, the emotional or romantic heart and the energetic heart, as in the heart chakra, is immense. It has so many roles to play and is truly what gets us through and sustains us throughout life. It is worth noting that anything that is manifesting or presenting on the physical level, will have a mental, emotional and or spiritual aspect and quotient to it as well.

We do ourselves a great service on every level when we decide to take care of and drop into the heart space. Sometimes we may need to clean up our heart space. In turn, we do great service to others too, for in addressing these aspects of the heart we become more present. Being more present, means we are willing to reveal our authentic nature and allow ourselves to open to others.

The heart appears to close, to shutdown or to block when we experience events, circumstances and traumas in our lives. What is nothing for one person may be the world for another. All is relative and all is valid. The death of a beloved, the ending of a relationship, the careless treatment from one to another, or the feeling of being left out because you were not picked for the team, can leave us feeling that our heart has broken, and in an instant, we feel it will never recover.

Indeed, such is our pain that our conviction that we will never recover, creates the attitude of *now I will close up this broken heart, so no one else will ever be able to break it and I will never ever feel this pain again.*

So we go about shutting down the heart in its broken state. We build barriers, moats and fortress walls, layer by layer, until all but the smallest chink is left, for one small ray of light to shine in and out. Satisfied that we have done a good job, we convince ourselves that we can now get on with life. On the outside we put on a mask to convince others, and yet internally we are still carrying that pain we have locked up inside. Interestingly, we convince ourselves, that because it is safely locked up, that it will go away, disappear or simply no longer affect us anymore. How wrong can we be!

To keep something closed up requires incredible amounts of energy. To keep our hearts closed up, with whatever is inside it, locked away and deeply buried, requires great strength, attention and energy. Even when it's done on automatic it means that a large part of us, is with that fortress deep within and is still with that event, circumstance or trauma. Some part of us is still with the others in the story, and all of that means, we are not present in the here and now, to the fullness of our own ability. Little wonder energy is low, and life is lacking in lustre and vibrancy. The physical body presents illness and disease. The mental body finds it hard to focus and often feels like it is in a fog just going through the motions. The emotional body is restless, dead or flying off in all directions, and the spiritual body seems remote to say the least.

We cannot be alive while we are avoiding life and shutting down our hearts, dulling down and denying that anything is wrong in the first place. When we are holding onto something, we are not able to take up the new with two free hands. First we must put down the old, only then will we have the space, energy and strength to pick up the new.

There is little to be gained from placing the new over, or on top of the old, for we will only perceive and experience the new through the filters of the old. We actually need to put the old to one side, so that we can move freely towards the new. This action can indeed be challenging for the old story, however unpleasant and painful, has become familiar and comforting. Much has been invested in keeping it just so. Letting it go can be a mountainous step.

To transfer the strength, the energy and attention that we have exerted over the years to keep all this in place, and to redirect it to the present, and therefore impact on the future, can be easily done. It requires willingness and intention. A willingness to transform what was, to change from the known, to step into the unknown and to allow. It requires intention, for energy follows thought. Clear intention acts as direction for energy. If our intention is to free up ourselves and our heart, so that we can flow with the energy of life, then that is what will begin to happen. If our intention is to stay exactly where we are, that is what will happen, even if later we get catapulted out! There are times that the higher self has other plans for us.

If our heart is scattered all over the world, it is impossible for us to be truly present. Love stories and legend talk about when falling in love you give someone your heart. To fall in love, implies or sets up the field for a falling out of love, a cycle if you like. To give someone our heart when we need it ourselves seems dramatic, and yet we have most likely all done it, at one point or another, to a greater or lesser degree.

When we are a new born and we look at our parents, an exchange of hearts occurs. We are in a dependent relationship, a codependent one especially wth our mothers, if they are breast feeding, and we need to be to survive. We forget to re-exchange hearts later on, creating space for an interdependent relationship to unfold. This inital heart exchange with our primary carers sets up a pattern of heart exchanges in many other relationships.

Our hearts are ours, to feed and sustain us first and foremost. Then it is possible for them to open and share with another. This creates a third synergetic heart energy that flows between people, creatures and everything. It is that synergetic heart energy that creates the energy of relationship. Stop giving the heart away, it's for us to keep, to nurture us, to fill us up with so much, that the overspill nurtures and feeds everything and everyone else we meet.

Reclaim the heart from everywhere it's been left and start building the most vibrant nurturing energetic powerhouse imaginable. Jean M Nadeau, a friend, suggested this process for me and I in turn have extended and developed it, and gone on to share it with him and many other friends, clients and groups around the world.

Once again, my greatest teacher comes into the picture, amazing how an animal can unravel your best built defences. Peri was a gift in more ways than I can begin to describe. He was literally a gift, given to me by a neighbour and friend at the time a fiveyear long relationship came to an end. My friend's motivation was heartfelt. *"You're my neighbour and a friend and you are a woman living on your own. If you have a dog you'll never have any problems."* (Alem, Said. 1998)

I had always considered myself to be a cat woman so I went into a bit of resistance over a dog. It took me a few weeks to move out of that and when the gift giver finally said, *"look you don't have to take the dog, but I bought him for you so you at least have to meet him.*

Then if you don't want him, lots of other people do." (Alem, Said. 1998)
So I agreed to go over and meet the dog

Little did I realise what I was stepping into as I went round the corner to his house, while he was out and his assistant let me in. Then magic came into play. As I stood in the living room, a little brown nose, followed by two big brown eyes and a ball of white fluffy fur, appeared from beneath a big rattan arm chair.

I stood stock still and watched my heart do a spiral horizontal dance to his and his do the same towards mine. It was just like in a Walt Disney cartoon, except this was real. That the hearts crossed somewhere in mid air I did not track. The deed was done just like that, in a blink of an eye, and the puppy came right up to me. I accepted that this was indeed the puppy dog for me. It was the end of 1998 and Peri, the Angel dog, had arrived in my life.

A week later, once the garden in the new house was finished, Peri moved in. It was later that his name came through when a friend came to visit. In full his name Peridot, is after the crystal, reflecting its properties of joy, loyalty and playfulness.

It was through sharing this part of our story with Jean that the next piece opened for me. My friend shared an observation. He had noticed that when a woman had a boyfriend, her heart was unavailable and then he had also noticed the same energetic quality that when a woman had a pet they were closed as well. The heart was closed, unavailable to others and directed elsewhere. Naturally this applies to both men and women. Jean had felt this energetic in me when we had first met and assumed I was in a relationship. Now knowing me better, he felt to share the observation and suggested that I simply re-exchange hearts with Peri. From this a process was born.

Reclaim your Heart is simple to do and transforms codependency in to interdependency. It is a disentangling and it is done by you for yourself, with gratitude and yes, it affects the other. It is not something you do to or on anyone else. The intention is to reclaim your heart and in doing so you create a space of willingness, of interdependence, of allowing, freedom and peace. Prior to the process there is often a frequency of control, codependency, neediness, obligation, even restriction and stuck-ness. In some cases, possibly also the frequency of anger, resentment and suffering may be in the field. Forgiveness frequently arises.

Settle in to a quiet space where you will not be disturbed by anyone or anything. Phones, computers and such like, all removed for the duration. This process is done from a space of gratitude and love. It is done from a feeling space and I recommended that time is taken to really feel what each step feels like. Rushing through the process renders it ineffective and little will shift or transform as a result.

Many interesting things can happen, so it is important to stay focused and follow each step as it is written. If something unexpected happens, stay focused and come back to the step you are on. Stay with it until it is completed, before moving on to the next step.

Sit comfortably and rest with your breath. The process is conducted in your mind's eye, where it can take place on an energetic level and from a more balanced consciousness.

Then when you are ready, call up the other, be that a person, animal, project or country and see them or sense them, standing before you, in your mind's eye.

Begin by thanking them for having been in your life.

Thank them for all the gifts that their presence in your life, has brought to yours, even if some of them have been painful or challenging, and even if you can't quite see all the gifts yet.

Thank them, for you know, on some level of consciousness, that there are many gifts.

When you are complete be silent and still. Then listen with an open heart and an open mind.

Let them speak to you, from that same space of gratitude and love. Let them thank you for being in their life, for all the gifts you being in their life has brought to theirs, even if some of them may have been painful or challenging.

Let them thank you for all the gifts, even if they haven't quite seen all of them yet. They too know there are many gifts and they thank you for them.

They will speak to you, so be open to receiving what they have to say. Sometimes we hear the actual words and at other times we get a sense of the gratitude and love. Sometimes we just get a grunt or a nod. Accept whatever comes.

We can always find something to thank someone for, so take time and allow gratitude to arise.

Once this step is complete say clearly "I now give you back your heart." And do so. Allow any emotion that arises to be present. It will pass and you will feel something go. Do whatever you need to do to give the other back their heart, even if that means putting it down beside them. Take time to complete this step.

With the next step it is important to note you are stating a fact and then doing the action. This is not an apology or a request.

Then tell them "I now take back my heart" and do so.

There is no room for negotiation here, none. Note you give their heart back first, so they have something to hold onto and then you take back yours. Again, this can bring up emotion. There are times we give our heart away when we are in pain, so taking it back means we are going to experience that just for a moment. It is ours, so allow it to be there and it will pass. Feel your heart filling up in the space you have created.

The next piece still requires courage and compassion. Face each other and sincerely and genuinely wish each other well. Take the time to feel this.

Then turn towards the horizon and walk individually, separately and in opposite directions, into the most beautiful sunrise you can imagine. A sunrise is symbolic of new beginnings.

This step is the resolution of what has gone before and an opening of the space for what may now arise of its own volition. It is an acknowledgement that what was is now complete, and what may come, is now allowed. We are saying goodbye to what was in order to say hello to what can be, in a different energetic.

Finally sit and be still within the space that you have now created. Both parties are now free to be wherever they are meant to be and wherever is best for them to be. Any further interaction, if there is to be any, will be out of willingness rather than out of need, obligation or dependency. Willingness carries with it a lightness of being and the energetic of joy. The other will also feel the shift. There is no need to test the result. What has occurred has occurred energetically. Trust all is well.

I recommend that you refrain from contact with the other for a full day following the process. In an especially challenging situation perhaps leave a longer gap of two or three days. That means refrain from opening text messages, taking phone calls or opening emails.

This is a very liberating process and it changes the dynamic between people, animals, projects and places in a subtle, clear, healthy and compassionate way.

An additional step can come in for a deeper and extended process. It is not always appropriate or necessary, so only use it if it resonates on a situation by situation basis. There are times when we have taken on attributes from the other person or object, which do not serve or belong to us. For example, we can take on the expectations, fate, fears and emotions of our parents or partners. Likewise, we may have given other aspects of ourselves away, aside from the heart, such as our dreams, visions, creativity, spirituality, self confidence, trust in the process of life, in relationships, our motivation, our joy and so forth. It may therefore be important and empowering to reclaim them as well.

This additional step occurs after you have reclaimed your heart. Then you can give the other back what ever you have taken on from them, one by one, with gratitude and grace. As you do so, you will feel yourself become lighter and lighter. This is followed by you taking back what you have given or left with them, one by one, with gratitude and grace. As you do so, you will feel yourself to grow in strength and presence. Always give back their heart and reclaim your own heart first, before you reclaim any other aspects.

Then wish each other well and walk into a beautiful sunrise.

Frequently reclaiming the heart is enough. In exceptional cases you may need to do more. Trust your intuition on this.

After my conversation with Jean, I resisted doing it immediately, for fear of loss entered the field. What if I did this and then Peri disappeared or died? However, when I woke up at 03:00 a.m, I decided to do it right away. Peri was asleep outside the bedroom door. As soon as I began, the tears welled up and the walls around the heart began to soften.

Peri came into my life at a time of intense heartache, sadness and metaphysical death, when a long term relationship came to an end. It was a time of profound transformation. As I began to thank Peri for all the gifts he had brought to my life by being in it, all of this came flooding back and the residue of whatever was left now had space to move.

I listened as amazingly Peri said whatever he wanted to say to me. It wasn't actual words, but a sense of gratitude and incredible unconditional love that came through. Then the hard part and I really did find it hard. I gave Peri back his heart and sobbed royally as I did so. Now, what was I going to do? My heart space was dark, cold and empty.

I waited and then I told him, "I now take back my heart."

At first I felt nothing. It was as if there was nothing there and I felt just a little scared. Then a small flicker and the realisation that I had given Peri my heart when it was battered, bruised, bloody and broken, metaphysically speaking, and I had taken his, which was vibrant, lively, playful and joyful. I had wanted to get rid of my heart. Or at least give it away, so it could be healed for me. It was however my heart, and now that I had it back the old pain could start to dissolve. It was for me to heal, and to bring it and myself, more fully back to life.

The gratitude was overwhelming as we wished each other well and then walked separately into the sunrise. All felt at peace. Invigorated I decided to do the process with a few more people and then fell back to sleep.

At 06:00 a.m. ready for a morning run, I opened the door and felt the energetic shift and transformation between Peri and I. There was an added lightness in his step, a brightness and a twinkle in his eye, and more cheekiness in his play. I also felt lighter, brighter and fuller. There was an ease between us. It was amazing, instant and it was here to stay.

Each time I facilitate this process for another I am honoured to witness the most heartfelt transformations and freedom created on all sides. I have extended the process to include animals, countries, places of work and even things that people have become attached to, be it to their projects or to material things.

I also recommend that those in a relationship reclaim the heart, so that they continue to be in a relationship out of willingness rather than out of need and obligation. I suggest parents do the process every once in awhile, in relation to their children, again to create a willingness within their relationship, freeing up both parties to be themselves and to do what is right for them. The list goes on; siblings, school friends, people who have died, ex-loves, enemies, colleagues, special places and so forth.

The more integral we are with ourselves and the more of our hearts we reclaim and bring back to the here and now, the more we are able to feed and nurture ourselves. Then the walls can come down and our heart can open and radiate, just like the Lotus flower and gradually connect with other open hearts, creating a third energy that then radiates out to others. The more present we are with ourselves, the more present we can be with others. The more present and alive we are, the more presence can radiate from us and the more vibrant and dynamic our lives can be.

In an energy-based fractal universe, where patterns repeat themselves ad infinitum, we will energetically attract a 'vibrational' match. Start to emit that which you wish to experience. We can be fully in our hearts. We can operate from that space and experience a world of compassion. Experience the world through the matrix of love.

This leads us to being in a better position to begin to generate and indeed manifest the possibility, potential and actuality of relationships between equals. Disentangling ourselves to bring forth, encourage and support the open heart, allows us to develop personal responsibility for "self" and to coexist, in an authentic and balanced way with others. It is a gift we give to ourselves and others. It is a gift we contain, and it is there waiting for us, at any given moment that we choose to let go of the past and to step into the present. This in turn creates a flow for a different future.

When we stop giving our hearts away or leaving them in distant places, when we stop making others responsible for our condition, and when we allow the fragmented self to reintegrate, the power of the victim identity starts to diminish and eventually dissolves. As this happens, the humanitarian and ethical aspects of the human being can begin to emerge and shine.

Authentic relating can begin to occur just by becoming more present. Recognition of how interdependent we all are upon each other, as well as, on the planet, opens the way for greater respect and a willingness to flow in exchanges of all kinds. It is said that it is our nature to connect and to relate. So let's begin by relating to ourselves, from the heart and relating to others as the hearts meet in the space of peace, freedom and trust. This is the art of allowing ourselves to be who we be.

Supported, nurtured and guided by all of our heart allows others to be and do the same. Control winds down, fear diminishes and co-creation can begin to flourish, for the highest good of all. Reclaim your heart, reclaim yourself and allow forgiveness to be given space to unfold.

Twelve

Forgiveness

*"Forgiveness is opening the door to opportunity for
things to change."* (Tutu 2004)

Forgiveness, like everything else in life, begins and ends with us.
Forgiveness is a gift we give to ourselves and one we share with
others. Forgiveness is what will help our hearts to open. It is what
will help us to become unstuck, to start to flow like the freshest
purest water in the mountain stream. Forgiveness is one of the
essential ingredients to living a life fully. Forgiveness opens the
way for unity.

As we reclaim our hearts and aspects of ourselves, forgiveness
frequently arises. When forgiveness is missing from the frame,
things within us begin to shrivel up, contract and die. That is
the fear matrix at work. This is then reflected back to us in the
external world, as our attention focuses on those things which
are also in a state of un-forgiveness, such as when others are
expressing defensiveness, aggression and brutality. Or when all
we see around us, is shrivelled up and dead.

This state of un–forgiveness creates such a metaphysical block
within the heart centre, that it can well impact physiologically
upon the heart, the other organs and cells within our physical
being. The work of Dr Masaru Emoto, *The Hidden Messages in
Water*, on water crystals, gives us a vivid view into the impact that

our thoughts and feelings have upon energy forms. Remember, we are 80 per cent water.

Whatever we think or feel, we are having an impact upon our internal state, as well as, projecting that out and having an impact on the external environment around us. We are in one vast energetic space where each of our individual fields, bounces into others and impacts the collective consciousness centres. This is why every time someone alters their perceptions and beliefs about themselves or others, they simultaneously change the structure of mass consciousness for us all.

Physicists, psychologists and socio biologists, such as Nassim Haramein and Dr Bruce Lipton explore this interconnectedness in great detail. Something we already know intuitively is now being scientifically explored and found to be true. It is time for all of us to look within and without, and to respond to the best of our ability, to what we find, by cleaning up our own world. This is taking personal responsibly for what we are creating in our lives and in the lives of others.

We are all capable of forgiveness. We talk about it a lot and we say that we do it, but do we really? Forgiving another maybe thought of as the biggest challenge and the place to start, it is however, taking us away from the source of un-forgiveness. That source is actually us. We need to forgive ourselves first, before we can even begin to come close to forgiving the other. This holding on to the hurt, the resentment, the secrets, the shame and the guilt, which are hidden under the un-forgiveness, results in all kinds of 'illnesses'.

Our physical, mental, emotional and spiritual facets are totally interconnected and we need to address all aspects to free ourselves from fear, so we can step beyond it into love. It is as we forgive ourselves that something magical begins to occur. As Rev. Desmond Tutu said, at the Global Community Peace Conference, held at the Arma Museum, Ubud Bali in 2004, *"Forgiveness is the answer and the future of our self interest means it is worth it"* (Tutu 2004)

First I look at what forgiveness is not. Then at what is actually meant by forgiveness, and at the different effects that may arise. Finally, I present a simple and profound process, which gets the mountain stream clean and clear from within, so it can refresh the world outside.

Forgiveness is not making the others right and ourselves wrong.

Forgiveness is not making ourselves right and the other wrong.

Forgiveness is not about blame.

Forgiveness is not saying what you did or what I did was okay.

Forgiveness is not going to make the past disappear.

Forgiveness is not going to delete or erase what happened.

Forgiveness is not about becoming best friends with the other.

Forgiveness is not about forgetting or sweeping something under the carpet.

In contrast

Forgiveness is about reclaiming ourselves and freeing the other. In doing so, we receive and give the gift of freedom.

Forgiveness is about reclaiming our power and transforming ourselves and the other.

In doing so, a rebirth occurs.

Forgiveness is giving up all hope for a better past.

In doing so, we become present.

Forgiveness is making a conscious deliberate choice to no longer carry anger, resentment or hurt within our psyche. In doing so, we improve our health.

Forgiveness is a decision to forego the desire for revenge. In doing so, we become more peaceful.

Forgiveness is declaring to ourselves and the universe "I am willing and I want to be at peace, laying to rest the old stories." In doing so, we allow things to change.

Forgiveness is reaching out a hand to All That Is. In doing so, we step into grace.

As we forgive, the heart breaks, the tears flow and the heart opens a little wider. Love can start to grow. As the walls soften and crumble, a state of grace begins to unfold. We reveal our own beauty and light to ourselves and to the world.

Forgiveness requires that we drop our sense of self importance.

To remain in the state of un-forgiveness requires a lot of energy. To stay in that state will impact upon the health of an individual with heart attacks and cancer. It will impact on the health of an institution, manifesting as inefficiency and incompetence. It shows up in the health of a country in the form of unrest, civil disturbance and war. Ultimately it affects the health of the planet creating a toxic environment.

That demise in health occurs as the energy ceases to flow and becomes stuck in a whirlpool of emotion, resistance and desire. It requires time to stay in that state. It's a way of saying I am not going to be present in my life. I am not going to be present with myself or with others. I am going to have part of me locked up in the past, recreating it again and again and again in the psyche.

This makes us unhealthy and we frequently get sick or experience disease. That will then require time and resources to address. Money is often spent in large amounts on prescription drugs, on alcohol, on psychotherapy, on operations, on street drugs, on all sorts of things which have arisen in the physical from the mental, emotional and spiritual dis-ease of holding ourselves in a state of un-forgiveness.

To move gradually and gently into a state of forgiveness, requires energy, time and inner resources. Energy, so we can direct our attention to the present. Time, so we can sit with what is, allowing ourselves to do the forgiveness process and experience all that it brings. Inner resources of courage and vulnerability, for these will stand on either side of us, as we do the process to reclaim ourselves and our energy, expanding our heart and connection, to the eternal well spring of our being.

This process can assist us in becoming more present in the present, which after all, is all we have right here, right now.

It is not something to be rushed through or got through. It is crucial to meet ourselves exactly where we are and to go as far as we are able, willing and ready to go. Often the layers of un-forgiveness around a person, situation or event have taken years to accumulate, and although for some it is possible to let go all at once, it is more common for us to take our time and do it piece by willing piece.

Do not fall for the "oh I'm not ready yet" resistance and avoidance pattern that can kick in. Integrate the one piece that can be done that day and then the next day do a little bit more. Each day you will find that you can go in just a little bit further and create more space for yourself. Slowly and surely your relationship to yourself, to what occurred and to the other, will alter in ways you cannot expect or control. Forgiveness has its own way of revealing yourself to yourself and guiding you into a state of grace. Allow it to do so and be enthralled and grateful for where it takes you.

The process below was shared with me by a colleague and dear friend, Frederique Nault. There have been many occasions when I have used this process personally and also when coaching others. I found this highly effective for addressing the situation when I was bitten by the two Rottweiler dogs. I will present the process first and then illustrate how I used it in my situation.

Create a quiet space so you can honour the gifts the forgiveness process will bring. Turn off the computer, the phone and anything else that may disturb you. Ask for time out from family if necessary.

Put your attention on a situation or event where you recognize that you are in state of un-forgiveness. Be clear what the situation is and only take one situation at a time. At times it may involve a person or people, at others a place of work or a country. All are possible. Do the whole process through to the end, before stepping back to the start. Remember it is a feeling process rather than a thinking process, so take all the time needed. Naturally, personal integrity is important. For the process to be of most benefit, create a calm space externally and internally. Make sure you feel cented and grounded. Stay with the process and follow each of the steps through to completion.

Take a few long slow breaths and feel the situation. Close your eyes, if that makes it easier to drop into the space.

1/ Forgiveness of self

We are forgiving the self we were at the time, that somehow or another, found itself in the situation concerned. We are looking back and viewing who we were then, from who we are now. The gift of hindsight is huge. Use it well.

Be kind and gentle. Remember we did not know then what we know now. We were often doing what we felt was best for us at the time. We may have felt we did not have a choice; we may have been reacting rather than responding. View the being that we were, with a non judgemental eye, like a benevolent parent or guardian viewing a child. From that space, breathing in love and breathing out love, start extending forgiveness to that self.

It is important to take time to just sit and be with that, without response.

Self judgements and criticism may arise. Recognise them, spot them, stop them and drop them. Those judgements and criticisms keep us separate from ourselves and others. The judgements keep us locked in the vacuum of the past, and in the state of un-forgiveness.

If we can forgive ourselves for being human, for not knowing how it would turn out, for feeling scared, for feeling stupid, for not telling the truth, for being shy, for whatever it is that comes up, then that is a start. Remember it is not about doing it all in one day, though once we get started we may well wish to do it all.

When you are ready to begin, call up the self that you were at the time of the situation and hold that self in the mind's eye. Remember that self is the small one and you are the big one.

Tell the smaller self, how grateful you are to see him/her. Tell them, how much you have missed them.

Tell him/her that you are here today to say how sorry you are that you were unable to be with them, when they needed you most, with the knowledge and the awareness that you have now. Sincerely apologise.

Tell him/her that you love them and that if he/she feels they need it, you forgive them for their perceived wrongness. Take time to tell the smaller self what it is you feel he/she really needs to hear from you. Forgive them for being a human being and learning about life. Allowing this in ourselves helps us to allow it in others as well.

Extend forgiveness to them and invite him/her to come back into your heart.

Negotiate a little if he/she is a bit hesitant about reintegrating into the whole, by asking what he/she needs from you to feel comfortable to do so. Honour any agreement, made between you both, in real time over the next few months. Perhaps you have agreed to walk in the park more often. Make sure you do it at least once or twice a week.

Once both parties are more comfortable and at ease, if it feels appropriate give each other a big hug. Then bring the smaller self up to the heart space and placing your hands over your heart, enjoy the feeling that that brings. Stay with it for as long as feels good.

2/ Forgive the other or others

Now bring your attention to the other. There may well have been more than one person involved however, so take them one by one in this step.

Forgive the other for who they were at the time that the situation occurred, not for who or what they are now or have become in your mind over time.

Stick as closely to the facts as you can. Remember you are viewing who or what they were then. They may have been coming from the feeling that they didn't have a choice. What occurred is often what may have seemed best, from a place of not having a choice or from reacting rather than responding. Take time to see that being, institution or country, with a non judgemental eye, like a guardian viewing a child, breathing in love, breathing out love and gradually extend forgiveness to the being or object of un-forgiveness.

Forgive them for being a human being and learning about life.

You may well need or want to do this step by step, a little bit at a time. The anger and resentment, the hurt and the pain you have felt, indeed still feel, and the suffering you have endured and therefore feel towards this being, may take some time to dissolve and fall away. Meet yourself exactly where you are and forgive them for being human, being hurtful and being all the things that come up. Take them one by one, for these are the judgements and criticisms that keep you in a holding space, locked up in the event in the past and disconnected from yourself and others. Likewise it keeps them in a holding space as well.

Again, do as much as you feel able to do at this time, knowing it is possible to do the whole process again and to come back to it again and again, until there is nothing left in the space except for forgiveness. Once you get started you may want to just keep right on going until you reach that space. Listen and follow your heart.

3/ Forgive the situation

This step may be a little easier now that step one and two have been experienced.

Circumstances and events seem to create situations and these are also harboured inside, in that well of un-forgiveness. The well is steeped in anger, resentment, sadness, hurt, pain, fear, disappointment and suffering. Our holding on to that, keeps part of us in the story of the past, wishing it hadn't been like that and wondering what would have happened if.

These are indications that we are still wishing for a better past. Forgiveness is letting go of all hope for a better past and that includes the "what if's." Breathing in love, breathing out love, extend forgiveness to the situation accepting it just as it is, just as it was, for you are not changing what happened, you are changing how you view, perceive and respond to it.

Watch however, for all the hopes and wishes for it to have been different and if they arise take them one by one, forgiving the elements that appear to have made up and contributed to the situation on an external level.

For example, the family, the economic down turn, the natural disaster, the civil war or the political situation, the hospital policy and so on. The external forces over which you feel you had no control.

If feelings of helplessness arise, recognise and acknowledge it as a feeling. It is not you, it is just a feeling. Say to yourself, 'Helplessness is present I forgive myself for identifying myself with this feeling of helplessness, I forgive this feeling for being present. I accept this feeling as it passes through me and I let it go.'

In this step we are forgiving the external world as perceived by us and we may well experience the sensation of being at the mercy of things outside of us. The feelings of helplessness, injustice and "it's not fair" may well come up. Do not go into them. Forgive them and come back to forgiving the situation itself, until you can just be with the situation in a state of forgiveness.

A clear uncontrived neutral will gradually arise. It may transform into gratitude at a later stage. This is what happens when we can see the gift of the situation and are ready to receive it for what it was, a gift.

4/ Forgive the Creator

In this step the creator means whatever it means to you. Notice any reactions and responses that come up and breathing in love, breathing out love, extend forgiveness to the creator. Extend forgiveness through each and every one of the reactions and responses.

Take your time with this one as it can be more significant than your mind may like to think. It can be surprising how much anger surfaces at this point, especially if we believe we do not believe in any ultimate creator, outside of ourselves.

Of course that would mean we have created it all and that would be stepping into a new level of personal ownership and responsibility without a doubt. Do as much as you can. Meet yourself and the creator of the whole story, right where you are, right here, right now. Be willing to be surprised.

5/ Wash away any residue of un-forgiveness.

This last step is to flush out any pieces you may have been reluctant to address, at which ever level or layer you are at or indeed the whole story if you have decided to go for it all. To do this you can call upon your higher self, the purest form of all light, spirit, whatever terminology works best for you.

With intention ask for that energy to wash through you, taking with it any residue of un-forgiveness and returning it transformed to source. Stay with this part of the process for as long as you can, until peace begins to fill every cell, every particle and every atom of your being, with such healing loving energy that you feel clearer, lighter and brighter.

Trust your intuition here and your sense of your own state of being. You will know if you need to go through the process regarding the same situation again or not. If you do need to, then set a fixed time and a date within a week to come back and do the next piece. Be kind and gentle with yourself for the next few days and watch what unfolds. Be aware that such a process can trigger a detox, on a physical, mental, emotional and or spiritual level. It could be a combination, so stay in observer role and drink plenty of water to ease the clearing.

If you feel complete, trust it, you will know. You can, to my knowledge, expect to sense and perceive the world in a brighter and clearer way. Those around you will be more responsive. They will seem to be more open, friendly and loving towards you.

Suddenly life will seem to be flowing and things will be easier. What once was stuck can move. You may even feel your heart and chest area physically expand and that the physical body itself feels healthier, more flexible and mobile. The world is a reflection of you and it is a perfect way to gauge how much of that sate of un-forgiveness has dissolved.

It is important to note we do not need to find the person, institution or country and go and be with them. What has occurred has occurred energetically. We do not need to test it. Trust how you feel inside and let the rest of it just be as it is.

The effects will be felt and if it is for you to cross paths again, that will occur without any effort on your part what so ever. What you experience then, will be whatever it will be. There is nothing to know, nothing to do, nowhere to go. For now just be. There are times when we may need to do the forgiveness process to free up even more space, having already reclaimed the heart. At others we may need to do the forgiveness process first, to be able to fully reclaim the heart. Trust your intuition and follow what feels right to you.

In my own case I found this process very useful in clearing any residue of resentment and un-forgiveness I felt towards the situation where I had been bitten by the two Rottweilers. Looking back at that situation a few years on, I noticed that I had yet to fully forgive myself for the betrayal of my own knowingness. I had betrayed my intuition. Step one allowed me to recover the aspect of me that had fragmented off when I judged myself in this situation.

I forgave myself, the self that I was then, who was acting without the awareness, knowledge and experience that I have now. At the time, I thought I was doing what was right and I was operating through the disease to please.

In step two, in my situation I needed to forgive my hostess, each dog and the host. I took each one separately and only when I felt at peace did I move on to the next other. With my hostess for example, I saw her for the being that she had been at the time. As a human being doing the best that she could at a time when her life was in pieces. She had a dinner to finish preparing and time was running out. Her attention was on the dinner and holding her heart together. Her action was not directed towards me, even though it affected me. It was not about me.

When I could recognise my hostess as a being in pain and that her turning back into the kitchen was a natural response, given her awareness at the time, I could begin to soften and extend forgiveness. She, like me didn't realise what she and I now know. I took the same approach with the dogs and the host, taking as much time as I needed.

In step three, forgiving the situation was easier having done steps one and two. In my situation I had been invited to Christmas Eve dinner with my hostess and as I was staying there, I felt obliged to be there.

For me the gift was starting to really see and clear the impeding self limiting beliefs and patterns of behaviour that I had been operating through.

In the fourth step, in forgiving the creator I received a surprise. Part of me was still holding on to my Catholic upbringing and the notion of God as the supreme, separate from me, creator. Another part of me recognised that I create my own reality and even if not consciously, this notion of the supreme creator is within me. I took time to handle all sides of that dynamic.

The final step was surrendering anything left in the field. Surrender is to choose to stop holding on to something, in this case un-forgiveness, with deliberate conscious awareness. It is deciding to change the act of grasping, into the act of opening and allowing. It is liberating and requires courage. Energy can once more begin to flow. We can come back to ourselves.

It is a myth that to surrender is a weakness. Surrender is not submission. Surrender is a choice. Submission in contrast, may be coerced through some use of force.

The gifts of forgiveness in my experience are gratitude, freedom, acceptance, allowing, presence and peace. Forgiveness brings us closer to ourselves.

As we move through the forgiveness process we start to see the gifts that have been hidden from view. At times we do not see that some action or event has actually been the catalyst for a positive occurrence in our life. A break up can actually be the trigger for us to step into our own power, onto our own path, and into becoming who we be today. A death or ending can be a new beginning, a rebirth or a journey into freedom. The lessons gained from events that happen in our lives are present and forgiveness helps us to receive them, and to be more present right here, right now.

As we forgive ourselves we are actually increasing our own levels of self acceptance. We are stimulating compassion towards ourselves and we are activating the heart for a greater love to flow. At such times that we can do this for ourselves, direct it towards ourselves and be open to receiving it, we are stepping back into the magical experience of being alive. We are creating space to connect.

Once we can really do this for ourselves we can then be authentically forgiving, accepting and compassionate towards others. We can complete the cycle. It starts and ends with us. Even though at times it may feel easier to forgive the other than ourselves, it is hollow, for without us in the picture nothing is really happening.

We are the one who is suffering and in pain. Allow that state of grace to unfold within and as our heart softens, it opens like a lotus in full bloom. It is time to treasure the precious gift that we can give to ourselves and then share it with others.

In this way, the world in which we live can begin to change, for we, within the world, are changing. As we continue to traverse the spiral of life, we can choose intelligent regret over guilt. We can choose forgiveness over anger and resentment. We can choose the matrix of love over the matrix of fear and live a life which can be something other than our current experience. We can let it take us beyond the known, to a place where anything is possible. Forgiveness opens the doors and the windows for the sun to shine in.

"Forgiveness says here is a new beginning possible" (Tutu 2004)

Forgiveness enables self acceptance to grow. It facilitates a letting go of our shadow selves with greater grace, gentleness and ease.

Thirteen

Dance of the Shadows

If we want to show up more fully and be ourselves that means accepting all aspects of ourselves. It means allowing our fragmented and hidden selves to be seen by us, accepted as us and then integrated by us. That way those aspects no longer need to play out on the world stage, show up in our communities or amongst our friends and families.

The dance of shadows and the impact that they have on our lives can be subtle and seemingly un-intrusive. Or they can be blatant and highly disruptive. A shadow side or shadow element, as I view it, is an aspect of ourselves which we deny, reject, resist and abandon. All of these actions result in its continued play in and effect upon our lives and therefore upon the lives of others.

The non-acceptance of self, figures heavily in this dance and is one worth addressing with gratitude, forgiveness and compassion. It will result in greater depths of self acceptance and assist us in stepping more comfortably and fully out of the matrix of fear and into the matrix of love.

The dis-owning of our shadows has a habit of showing up in other people who are in our lives, or who appear to be in our lives. Our dis-ownership means that we project them out into the world and we have someone else play them out for us. They might show up as the controller, the dictator, the killer and so on. It is impossible to become a more fully integrated being if we ignore the shadows. If we do so, we do so at our own peril. The world is coming from us.

Something doesn't just go away because we sweep it under the carpet, put it in a draw, lock it up and throw away the key. Our consciousness, however forgetful we may appear to be, knows where it is, all the time. Part of us is with it all the time, rather than being right here, right now in the present, which is our gift to ourselves and to others.

A denied, disowned or rejected shadow, as I see it, is similar to a young child wanting and vying for attention. Many will do whatever they can until they get what they want. It is not important what kind of attention they receive after a while, as long as they get some. A child really has few fundamental needs, once addressed life flows with more grace and ease. The fundamentals are; acceptance, love and affection, being talked to as a being with intelligence, being supported, being given a sense of their own place within the family, the community and the world and being given nutritious food and drink.

A structure, coupled with acceptance, in which to have a sense of boundaries and ethics, helps any being find their own place within the world. Acceptance as a child engenders acceptance of self and when someone is accepting of themselves, they are operating from the heart space, from the matrix of love and in greater balance and harmony within and with the rest of the world. Acceptance and integration of a shadow element will respond in the same way.

Acceptance is the key here and together with forgiveness and compassion, it flourishes and works hand in hand so to speak, to transform. We have created a world where self acceptance is in short supply, where the mass conscious belief of *not being good enough* and of *not being enough*, in whatever form it shows up, is a reflection of the low levels of self-esteem and acceptance. The cycle of the demise of a being, when low on self acceptance is easily seen in drug abuse, alcohol abuse, bullying, smoking, eating disorders, as well as, physical health, mental and emotional health and even in spiritual abuse. Addressing the shadow means dropping our judgements and experiencing self acceptance to some degree.

How can we begin to make a gentle step towards integrating our shadows, when we are in such denial? Well I did it the following way and present it as a way to start becoming more of ourselves.

First we look at the people who are currently in our lives.

Make a list of our family, a list of our closest friends and a list of our social friends. Next to each one we note down the traits we admire and like in them, and then write down what we are critical of. To do this, from a non spiritual identity, means that we allow what we really feel, to show itself to us. We do not need to be Ms or Mr Nice for this exercise. If we are, it will get in our way and highlight one of our shadows. Yes, you've guessed it, being Ms or Mr Horrible or Mean is one of our resisted identities and it is operating as a shadow in our life.

Our desire to be good, to be nice and to be acceptable, means that we do not actually feel like that but instead, feel the opposite. We repress it and it pops out somewhere else in the universe it all its glory. It shows up either in an uncontrollable outburst or by being imposed on another in our circle, or in the world. That being then becomes the very embodiment of Ms or Mr Bad. To handle our own shadow, is to liberate ourselves and to liberate others, from a lot of suffering.

Back to the lists, we put our attention on the traits we admire and celebrate those. What we recognise in another we have the seeds of within ourselves. It is known that if we can see and acknowledge a trait in another that it is there within us too, on some level and to some degree. We are mirrors and thus we are gifts to each other in this way.

It is something we are happy to do when the trait is viewed as being good and yet unwilling to do when the reverse is so. We are reluctant to accept that viewing the so called bad trait in another has anything to do with us and this is how the shadow dance gets played out with other people.

Take a moment to reflect on the traits which you do not admire within your family, close friends, and your social friends. Notice if there are any common traits or threads running through the list, reflect on whether the trait expresses itself in the same or different ways. Ask yourself if you are also like that and if you have ever been that way.

Allow that you to be present with the observing you, and become its guardian. Ask it what it needs and you will find very quickly that the bottom line is that it wishes to be accepted, to be loved and to know that it is safe. It usually wants to be invited to come back into the heart and to be part of the whole.

It does not take long to recognise what your shadow needs, though it takes courage to let it stand before you, to own it and to reclaim it as a part of you. It has fragmented out at some stage and it takes great compassion to bring it into a place where it can be comfortably integrated once more. Great compassion, from my limited understanding, contains love, acceptance, forgiveness and compassion all rolled into one, forming great compassion. This is the healing balm to be liberally applied to all the shadows and to all the wounds of the world.

There are times when it is necessary to cut a shadow off and to let it go completely. This can also be an act of compassion.

The family, friends and social circles we move in and the criticisms we make are the signals and sign posts leading us directly to our shadows. Perhaps we have a friend we always think of as weird or loud, another as a slob, yet another as uncouth, neurotic, psychotic, rude, flaky, selfish, self centred, a party animal. If we can name it, we've thought of it and labelled someone as it.

This is not limited to people. It can apply to places being dirty, hostile, inhospitable and dangerous. These are also elements of ourselves that we resist being and so constitute a shadow.

Work on the shadow or resisted parts of ourselves can bring up resistance and appear to block the process. The best approach to take is to dive right in to accepting the resistance first. A quick and effective process for resistance and shadow elements is as follows.

Own it as yours.

Accept yourself as it.

Forgive yourself as it.

Love yourself as it and let it dissolve.

We have chosen it. It comes from us and we need to recognize that even the denial comes from us. Handle the denial first using the following sentences. Remember this is a heart centred process, so we need to feel how it feels, rather than think how it feels. Allow time to drop into that space and feel the resistance. I used to be very uncomfortable with 'weird' and the feeling of being perceived to be weird. I'll take this as the example, yet choose that which is appropriate for you and your shadow. Then say each sentence and allow yourself to feel how it feels and where it sits in the physical body.

I choose to feel resistance to being weird.

I accept myself when I am in resistance to being weird.

I forgive myself when I am in resistance to being weird.

I love myself when I am in resistance to being weird.

I let it go and do so with gratitude and grace.

Then as you free up the resistance you can move into the process. Feel weird and then say each line.

I choose to be weird.

I accept myself when I am weird.

I forgive myself when I am weird.

I love myself when I am weird.

I let it go.

An extended practice, for those that wish to explore further, is to look to where you have felt like this in your life time and to see if you can traverse to the initial time. Be kind and gentle, there is no need to rush or push. Trust your intuition and allow the heart to guide you. The head will take you to interesting places, though not places you necessarily need to go to. Then go through the process once again and embrace all of those same shadows along the time line and integrate them into the heart.

Any one of these steps can bring us to our knees. It is a simple and profound process that will create changes on the inner and outer realms. Be prepared for physical shifts within the body, such as detox like symptoms. Our perception of and interaction with family, good friends and social friends out there in the world, will also undergo changes. Allow it to shift and transform at its own pace, acknowledging that there is a natural intelligence at work.

For me, the acceptance of my own weirdness freed up my fifteen year old so that she could integrate into the heart. I could finally see she was that way to get attention from her parents and to check out of unpleasant situations at school, where she felt not good enough. The acceptance also freed up my friend, who no longer needed to act out my shadow. My friend could now be viewed through one of the good traits I celebrate about them. Ultimately our friends can now be just as they are. Freedom of expression is in the field once more.

At times acceptance of our own projected shadow means that the person no longer needs to appear in our lives, and we will no longer attract that as a common characteristic or element in our world. It may show up a few more times, yet if we are quick to recognise it, own another layer of it and then start setting some clear boundaries, we will find that our good friends and social set changes, for we will no longer be a energetic match.

We start to attract other gifts and reflections into our lives, which will challenge us in other ways. Each and everyone is continually allowing another, as yet unmet or owned, side of ourselves to emerge. This is what is meant by we are everything and everyone.

We do not bring out the shadow so it can play out and wreak havoc on the world. We bring in the shadow so it can find its place within the heart and gradually the projected blame game can start to diminish. More authentic beings can have more authentic relationships, interacting with greater presence and love.

Significant relationships give us an incredible opportunity to discover, uncover and recover parts of ourselves for better or worse. Here is a great piece to use for cleaning up shadows in relationships that are sitting on our own side. This is a fun and liberating thing to do.

Make a list of your significant partners.

Next to each name write down what it was that attracted you to them.

Then write down what it was that most aggravated you by the end of the relationship.

Next cross check both lists and notice if there are any similarities.

Be prepared to be amazed. I noticed I was attracted to someone for their academic intelligence. Towards the end of that relationship I was aggravated by that same academic intelligence, which began to seem so cold.

If there are similarities, just for a moment recognise the play of desire and resistance and sit with it.

What once we have desired, we may also have aspired to be ourselves.

So now that we no longer aspire to be that way, we can catch a shadow hovering in the wings. As you review the partners' qualities from both the liked and less liked parts of the relationship, notice if there is a common pattern that runs through them all, as in all the partners.

Then do yourself and your future partners the service of integrating those shadow elements into the heart once and for all. There is little to be gained by pointing the finger of blame at the other, except for a repetition of the past and creating more pain and suffering. There is however, much to be gained. Experience the change within yourself and then what you experience with another. Move out of the shadow dance.

Relationships are present in everything we experience in life. The above process can be applied to any relationship where interaction occurs. Some relationships are deep, some are fleeting, others shallow and some are long lasting. Some are seen, acknowledged and recognised, others are unseen, hidden and kept secret.

There are also relationships that we ignore and do not view as a relationship, like the ones we have with distant farmers who grow the food we are eating and the transport drivers who deliver it to the places we buy it from. These, to all intents and purposes, are a relationship and they are the ones we give little or no thought and attention to.

It is however, these very ones that keep our world fluid. Our disconnectedness from them perpetuates our separateness in the world. To take the step of consciously recognising our interdependence of relationship to everyone and everything on the planet, is a small step with a potentially huge impact. The amount of gratitude in the world would increase to such a level that the matrix of fear would dissolve with greater grace and ease, and the matrix of love would flourish, as if by magic. Gratitude is a magical, yet very real element, worth nurturing in our lives.

The move away from the recognition that "we are everything and everyone," into "I am me and you are you" or "I am me and you are not me," leads us into a world of limited definitions. "I am this, I am not that." It is a world of polarities and dualities, a world of separateness, a world of "us and them," a world of "haves and have not's," a world of extremes and a world of disconnect. It is a world governed by the matrix of fear. It is the world we all too often find ourselves walking in today.

The next time there is a worker's strike for higher salaries and we find ourselves saying "they should stop complaining" or "they are being greedy" we can take that as a signal, to turn it back onto ourselves, and look for just a moment at where we just may be doing or have done the very same thing we are now judging the others for. If we are courageous enough to own it, we can then address that shadow side playing out on the national stage, and make our own contribution to changing the experience for ourselves and others.

It is the same if we address a shadow dance on the world stage. The "us versus them" in regards to terrorists for example, freedom fighters, rebel troops, repressive regimes and so on. We can do this by asking ourselves if we have ever tried to control another or others. Have we ever tried to impose our views onto another? Have we ever wanted to have it go our way? Have we ever said if I ruled the world? Have we ever said they should be killed? If we have, then it is time to step back for a moment and look at what we are saying, and what we are really doing.

Our shadow side has just appeared on the projected world stage and now we have an opportunity to dissolve our contribution to that play. Just use the five steps of owning it, accepting, forgiving, loving and letting go. For me this was triggered during an incursion by Israel into Palestine. As my criticism arose I pressed pause and looked within to see what I was resisting being. It was time I took my anger and resentment out of the collective field of energy that was feeding the very conflict I was so opposed to. My opposition to incursions anywhere in the world continues, yet rather than adding fuel to the fire, I seek ways to defuse the fire.

Relating in this way is about stepping into a different paradigm. Away from the "I factor" and the "what's in it for me" scenarios, we experience every day. The ownership of our resisted selves, our shadows in the wings, our acceptance, forgiveness and love of them, and ourselves, allows their integration into the whole. This enables the softening of the false divides, the illusory perceptions and the so called "selfish gene."

It creates an opening, a possibility for a new paradigm to emerge, to form and to take shape. There is an opportunity for a coming together, to move as one, in greater harmony and balance with the planet. When we do the work on the inner realms, we can see that as one person we can and do make a difference. We will experience the effects of what we do and this will gently and subtly, ripple out and touch all who know us, all who know them, and all who know them and all who.., and so it goes out to infinity. Combine that with a change in birthing practices and anything could happen.

We are all points of singularity in infinity and we all impact infinity. To become more consciously aware of what we think, who we be, and what impact we have, can be both daunting and exhilarating. Use it wisely and ask yourself what do I really, really, really want?

Whatever you really, really, really want is going to come from you, it is not going to come at you. You need to create it, and you do that in large part by how you treat and have treated yourself and others.

Embrace the shadow side and transform the world one shadow at a time.

Fourteen

Love and Mixed Messages

Love is an energy which generates and permeates everything and everyone. We simply don't see it because we are so busy looking for it, running from it or imposing it on other things or other people. We fill our lives with distractions and love becomes obscured. We artfully forget that it is the fundamental essence of ourselves. We breathe it in and we breathe it out, unconsciously most of the time. The body, which is our physical vehicle, is an expression of it, although all too often what we give it in return is toxic thoughts, toxic foods and drinks, and all manner of other things. Occasionally we may allow the body to be unfettered and pampered in a healthy way, yet that too is squeezed between rushing here and there.

The food we eat, notably those we grow ourselves and those that are grown organically, are grown from love. They are not intentionally poisoned. They are not forced to ripen. They are not forced to look, taste and be a certain way. They are nurtured and tended to by farmers who understand and move with the rhythms and the cycles of life. The way such food tastes, is different. The way it feels in our stomach is different. It supports life, for it in itself has vital energy and that means it is alive. In a sense we can taste love.

Walk into a well cared for garden and you will experience love radiating from all the plants, the trees and the creatures in the area. Things will grow more plentifully, more vibrantly and more quickly. Findhorn was created out of love and it has flourished to this day, even though it is in an inhospitable area. If that is the effect that love can have on one small piece of land, dare we even think about the effect it could have upon us if we would only let it. In a sense we can see the effects of love around us.

There are so many ways we say no to love, with *I can't or I'm not enough, or he, she, it is, not enough, or it should be, it can't be, I don't want it, I'm too busy, it is too scary,* and so on and so forth. Funny, that the life-giving essence, which is our very breath, is that which we deny, even though we crave it.

Love is not something that we find, it is what we are. Love is not something that we purchase through looking a certain way or having or doing certain things. All of that is conditional and rife with expectations and assumptions, which in turn means it is setting the ground for intense cycles of pain and suffering.

Love is not ownership that is possession. Possession is coming from the need to control, in order to feel more than and that is tied in with low self-esteem, which is an essential element of the fear matrix, and that is what stunts our growth.

Love may best be described by what it is not, for it is not a descriptive thing. Great poets and lesser ones, writers, artists, lovers, creatives of all kinds, have been at pains to describe what love is. Yet in words, we seem to be no closer to it and in the searching for it, the chasing away and the chasing after of it, we seem to push this elusive love so far away from us that we become lost in the stories in our heads, once more removed from the heart space.

Yet when we sit or walk in nature, allowing the sunlight to touch our skin in the early morning, the breeze to caress us and to listen to the water as it falls over the rocks and pebbles in a stream, we can get a sense of something beyond. As we see the dew on the tips of the leaves, on the blades of grass or the other crops, creating rainbows in the sunlight and as we watch the insects and other creatures go about their business, right there in the busy stillness of nature, right there, we might get a sense, a feel of something other than what we expect and it has no words, it just is and it makes us smile.

Something seems to soften and things look a little different. As they do, we begin to fill from the inside out, with such warmth that it makes us glow from head to toe. We expand and fill our space, extending out until we appear to touch everything around us, in harmony and balance. Within nature we can sense the magic and mystery of existence and of this thing we call love. For it is here, that a sense of rightness of place, is felt, known and celebrated.

In an urban setting, nature is still present, so find those places and be in them to allow that connection to come into play. It will do just that if you can give it the space to do so. A solitary activity, the energy of which, we can then take out into the community, society and world. We are energetic beings and we live in an energetic environment. That is to say, we are all made up of atoms, particles and quantum. We are energy. We are moving around in a sea of energy.

There are many books and works available on the market, which look at such things as the quantum field. There are books and talks by scientists and specialists, as well as, those who are well versed in sacred geometry, esoteric and religious teachings. Explore these further for more information on a scientific level. One that is well researched is, *The Field* by Lynne McTaggart.

As energy powerhouses, we are a little like a radio transmitter and a lot like a crystal. We do in fact have crystalline properties in the brain and these transmit and receive signals. Neuroscience is now catching up with something intuitive healers have known for a long time. Crystals emit energy. Cultures around the world have sought out and used precious and semi-precious gemstones or crystals for royalty, priests and for every other person within the nation.

If you hold a crystal loosely in the palm of your hand you will feel it. The feeling may be strong or weak, but you can feel it. Take a crystal that has been left out under the full moon and you will feel it even more strongly. Crystals are used for healing, be it in complementary medicine or in more conventional medicine. They are present in laser technology. Many people wear crystals and use amulets to feel better or for protection. Intuitively, we will be drawn to the crystals that are right for us at that time.

Feng Shui uses crystals to enhance a property, room or office, often with profound effect. Crystals have become common in many people's homes, and now crystal essences are being used as a vibrational medicine to address physical, as well as, mental and emotional issues. In my experience they work. Whether as a crystal in solid raw form, polished or made into an essence, they are powerful, and except for a few, that are not made into essences or elixirs, they are non-toxic and totally natural. When they have been radiated or heat-treated to enhance their colour however, rather like GM crops, they no longer contain anything nurturing in them and are more toxic than anything else.

Like crystals and radios, we are also transmitting signals and waves out to those around us. As we send out a signal, we receive a signal back in response. Dolphins and whales use their songs and sonar. Subconsciously we are doing exactly the same. The only thing is all too often we are sending out one message after the other, and they are contradictory. This can cause wonderful situations of misunderstandings, misconceptions and mixed messages, which in their extreme form can result in conflict and in their lesser forms, confusion and disappointment. That simply brings us back to pain and suffering.

If the pain and suffering has been created by us, so that we can more clearly see and experience joy, rather like dark reveals the light more clearly, then is for us to embrace it. It is also time that we see how we are contributing to and perpetuating it in our lives and the lives of others, and refrain from doing so.

Clarity of thought, action, word and deed, decreases the mixed messages emanating from each of us. The static on a poor radio signal means that we are catching only snippets of what is being said and frequently we are misinterpreting it. It is the same when we listen to people and when we interact with each other. It is a wonder we are able to communicate and get anything done at all really.

To tell someone "I'd like to see you, but I'm too busy" is a classic mixed message. "I'd like to see you," seems positive, yet it is followed with "I'm too busy," which really means "I don't want to see you." "Busy" carries with it a notion of self-importance or a fear of rejection that separates us from others.

Contrast the above with saying "I'd like to see you, can we see when we both have time to do this?" The first part is the same, and it is followed by an acknowledgement that the other person may also have time constraints. There is an absence of projected self-importance. The second part of the sentence contains a follow through which aligns with "I'd like to see you."

We are masters of contradictions. *I love you, but I hate you when you leave the TV on, drop the towel on the floor, leave the Wi-Fi on or leave the lights on in the car.* Whatever it is, it seems to be the small things that bring out the hate. So this is a great mixed message. *I love you, I hate you.* How can we know where we stand, let alone how can our loved one know where they stand with us? Hot and cold messages result in confusion, tension, and eventual conflict and separation. Is this love?

Another common example, someone asks, "is everything okay?" "Yes, yes, everything is fine." Clearly on some level the first person has sensed that something is not fine, yet the denial creates confusion. It is time to stop creating confusion and conflict within our lives and the lives of others. Eliminate those patterns that obscure our essence and act as distractions from what is really there.

Whatever you are feeling inside, no matter how good an actor or actress you are on the outside, someone will be picking up on the inner feeling. This means that the outer one will be perceived as being just a little bit off. To play a character convincingly, actors work to embody that character, leaving their own personality or character for a while and stepping into another. It requires great skill, discipline and courage to be able to step fully into and out of character.

If we can allow ourselves to be really true and honest with ourselves, we can allow love to begin to reveal its self, in and through us, for ourselves and others. When we keep ourselves trudging around in the quicksand of mixed messages we all get stuck. Relationships grind to a halt and we are left wondering why it didn't work out. Well, because we were one foot in and one foot out and no one knew where they stood, least of all ourselves.

What is it that creates mixed messages? Well ultimately it comes down to fear. For example the following beliefs may be coming into play:

If I show or tell someone how I'm really feeling they may walk away. Fear of rejection is present.

If I tell someone how I really feel about him or her, they may not feel the same and then I will look stupid or I'll be exposed and they will never talk to me again. Fears of how others view me, of rejection and of being alone, are present.

If I am too direct they will think I'm easy. Fear of being less than I should be, is present.

If I play hard to get they'll want me more. Fear of being less is present.

If I'm disinterested they'll come to me. Fear of how others perceive me is present.

Now where does all of that come from? When we like someone, we do and they can feel it. When we feel great, others feel it. When we feel blue, others feel it too. Perhaps it's time to stop being ashamed of our own feelings, of our humanness and to be brave enough to open up and to take what comes with honour and respect.

It may well be that another cannot be present with how we feel. At least by owning it we can become more accepting and present with how we feel, which means it can dissolve eventually. It may be that we like another and they do not feel the same for us. Accept that. However, pretending we do not like them is a lie and both messages are radiating out into the field.

When we acknowledge our feelings, without expecting anything in return, we can free the blocked field that lies between us, freeing ourselves to hear a truth and move towards where we actually need to be, rather than being stuck in a story in our head. If we still have expectations the field is not clear, and the expression of our feelings will most likely be laced with neediness and are therefore open to manipulation.

It takes courage to express what is really going on, even to ourselves. Courage because it requires vulnerability and risk, yet that courage brings with it trust. We can trust what we really feel and others can start to trust what they are sensing. Self acceptance and allowing unfold, for we can allow ourselves to be as we are and with this, others are given permission to do the same. This in turn leads to greater levels of peace within and externally, creating more space and harmony all round.

It doesn't matter if someone takes our expression of interest on a purely egotistical level. It's not important if they reject it. What is important is that we express it with grace, non-attachment and with compassion towards ourselves and the other. The relationship changes as a result, usually to becoming one of greater honesty and trust, more genuine and authentic. At the very least the relationship with ourselves changes, if not with the other. There is incredible freedom and we regain a sense of vitality and power in taking such action.

There was a man I had liked for a good year or more and yet had never had the courage to express myself. I had been too fearful to respond to his first advance and became skittish as a result. On subsequent meetings I'd be in and out of I like you, I don't like you. Little wonder he lost interest. I had been pretending not to like him to act cool, and because of that, I then got stuck in my story of actually liking him and wondering why he was distant.

After the realisation that my silence and secret were sitting in the field between us, making any real communication impossible, I knew a step up in integrity was going to be part of the action needed to open authentic communication once more. Fearful, I used kinesiology to check-in and see if I could simply do this energetically or if actually needed to talk with him. Well on this occasion, to free up myself and him, I needed to actually have a conversation and come clean. It was an opportunity to walk through the fear matrix. This is not always the case so be sure to check in first if you are in a similar situation. Most often an energetic reclaiming of the heart will be enough.

As uncomfortable as it felt at first, I took that step out of my comfort zone and out of the fear matrix. I heaved my heart into my mouth and as he was so kind to help me get started I went with it. I began by sharing that I'd been on a trip and I'd like to share it with him, for he had unwittingly been on it with me, in my head. Not sure where to start, he suggested the beginning perhaps, so as I laughed and things lightened I did indeed start from the beginning and shared what had been experienced, as coming from my own side.

When I was done, we spoke of love and he shared with me his view of love. It is like a power source, a battery pack, which we have inside of us. Sometimes as it fills we give it away to another, but actually we need to fill it for ourselves and keep it running over so that it can be felt by another. I was simply expressing for another, what I really needed to feel towards myself. I was projecting out what I needed myself. In speaking my piece, I reclaimed or redirected the energy of love to fill myself and overspill outwards to others, rather than running on empty and leaking it out to others.

Later that day, I got the confirmation that he had known all along, from a mutual friend. For myself there was a rush of energy, a sense of freedom, vitality and love. I loved everything I could hear, touch, see, taste and smell. I danced and everything felt lighter and brighter. Not only could I speak to him more freely but to everyone else as well. Our friendship grew from strength to strength, and continues to this day in a very genuine way.

This happens when we are totally free of attachment to the outcome. That means not even holding on to the tiniest bit of hope and being free of all hidden agendas. It is an act of allowing ourselves to be vulnerable. It is creating the space so that we can move through the fear of rejection, the fear of humiliation, even the fear of shame. Interestingly those fears are all ways that we block the flow of love. Cleaning up mixed messages is an act of taking full ownership of our story. It is this that is so liberating.

We let love move through us by allowing ourselves to clean up mixed messages. We can then become clearer as we transmit our presence in the world. Love can radiate from us and move towards us.

Fifteen

Follow your Heart

Follow your heart and give your head some time off. A different way of being and moving in the world will begin to unfold as a result, and it just may be increasingly magical and enchanting. When we decide we want to be ourselves, we will be asked to follow our hearts rather than our heads or what we think others would like or want us to do.

When I write follow your heart I am referring to general daily living, the activities we do and the decisions we may be required to make, rather than purely in the case of an attraction, a heart vow or an attachment to another being. In that situation, as in all others, it is important that we listen to our hearts and respect the feelings and wishes of others.

Motivation is a propelling force in our lives, and it is the difference between something occurring and something being a nice idea, yet postponed indefinitely. Motivation gets things done. However, to take some time out and reflect upon what our motivation is and where is it coming from, is an important step in any new undertaking.

There are so many "objects" which can motivate us. Resistance and desire are the basis of all of them and they are very powerful. It has long been known that a person will learn a new language more rapidly and effectively, if there is a mitigating and therefore motivating factor involved. At the most extreme level it is one of survival. Love or infatuation is also motivation, and then there is financial motivation, an opportunity for promotion, for a better job or for higher pay. Recognition can also be a major driving force behind people's decisions. There can be a desire to own certain things or to be able to move within a social scene and so forth. We may also be motivated from a hidden agenda or a subconscious desire to avoid something in our lives. All the above can deeply affect the decisions we make.

Frequently, when we follow our heart, having taken our own and others expectations and assumptions out of the field, our motivation no longer revolves around those former factors. In fact, much to the amusement of friends, family and colleagues, it has nothing to do with them and it may look, from their viewpoint, as if we have totally lost the plot. The decision may seem to be something close to foolishness or madness. Why else would someone walk away from a well paid secure position of work?

My decision to stop teaching and jump off into the great unknown is one such example. However, from the inside I knew I had to act upon that decision. I wanted to be true, and that was proving to be very challenging in the confines I had created at work. Whereas it was following that heart decision, through trial and error, ups and downs, that brought me to a place of deep inner peace and greater awareness, than I had ever had before. I'm extremely grateful for all the gifts along the way. Crazy as my actions may have seemed at the time to some and perhaps even still do, it was totally the right action for me to take.

I have no wish to paint a rosy and perfect picture here. Following your heart can be filled with times of uncertainty, insecurity and bleakness. Yet if we can ride through those, the growth we can experience and the freedom we can expand into, along with the treasures we open ourselves up to, are of such richness, that I would do it every time.

I have been privy to witness not only my own unfolding, when I followed my heart, but also those of clients I have worked with. There have been a few that stand out, when looking at motivation, as coming from the heart or the head.

A young woman came to see me, having experienced burnout at work. She had worked at the same company for over a decade, and was in a top position, earning a very good salary. The opportunity for promotion occurred, which would mean a fairly substantial increase in salary. The woman admitted that the new position did not actually interest her, but she did want the extra money.

Her primary reason was not because she actually needed it, she said, but because if she could have it, she'd take it as she'd be able to buy more things with it. Her second reason was because her partner was working less, so it would help to cover any emergency shortfalls. Interestingly, the young woman was coming from a subconscious fear of not having enough.

Less than six months into the new position, she felt out of her depth. Pride prevented her from asking for assistance. Fear of not looking competent enough, got in the way and she began to lose sleep and eventually went to pieces during a meeting with company heads. For the extra salary, the woman ended up losing her job in a company that had become her whole world. She had lost herself and her sense of connection to the outside world, and almost destroyed her marriage, her friendships and her social life in the process.

As it became clear to her that her decision to take the promotion was purely based on a head decision, for the extra income, and not a heart decision for how she could assist in the growth of the company, the realisation that she had become disconnected from her heart was unavoidable. The grief that followed was momentarily overwhelming, as there was within that one realisation, a revelation of the many other times she had overridden her heart and followed only her head.

Another client stumbled upon a hidden agenda during a lunch. She realised she had been pushing to go to a prestigious university, not as it turns out so she could study, but so she could hang out with the "cool, intelligent people." This realisation meant the client was now free to explore spending time with "cool, intelligent people" in a different way. Perhaps she could attend a summer course or weekly seminar. She could take the pressure off herself to be something she was not and allow herself to be who she really was.

Other cases, where people are wishing to leave their place of work, yet hold on for the annual bonus or commission are also common. Everyone wishes to negotiate for the best possible termination package, however the point to remember, is that we actually want to leave anyway. In many ways, once we have made that decision, we have already left.

To stay on so we can manoeuvre a better deal is out of alignment with our own integrity and with that of our employers. Ultimately we are putting off the inevitable. We are delaying our dream, and we are exhausting our spirit by overstaying our leave by date.

Our spirit has little interest in how much we have, what we do or who we know. Our spirit simply wants to be free to express itself to the highest potential of authenticity that it can. If we have a dream, we can plan it, prepare for it and do all the ground work, but until we actually let go of all the so-called security nets, we are living a controlled version of that dream, if we are even living the dream at all. It may well be a good, sensible, reasonable idea to have savings behind us, but when is enough ever going to be enough? If we don't have any savings in the first place then we have nothing to lose.

Motivation to do something, to be the best, as for athletes for example, or to become heads of companies, presidents and prime ministers, chief surgeons or teachers, nurses, taxi drivers or farmers, is all the same when coming from the heart. When coming only from the head, a different dynamic and use of energy comes into play.

This is especially so if the personality is so driven that they lose connection with that ethical side, and operate from an at any cost mentality. Underlying such behaviour is low self-esteem and it can be incredibly destructive to the self and others. People begin to operate using force, rather than being carried along by an inner power.

Drugs in sports for example, and sports men or women taking out contracts on their peers so they can be in the top position, the ice skater incidents in the1990's comes to mind. Business colleagues or partners, setting others up for failure by withholding vital information, so that others cannot carry out their duties or fulfil their commitments, are ways of undermining others in a company so that we can rise to the top.

To be the best at the deliberate cost, harm and destruction of others is clearly being motivated from something other than the heart. Ruthlessness and rising to the top no matter what the cost, is a paradigm that has been fed to many of us since we arrived on the planet. That mode of operating has contributed to the destruction of the planet, the breakdown of social and community networks, and the demise of altruistic humanistic traits. Why is it so celebrated?

However, when we are able to own that and move from the head into the heart, deliberately and consciously, we will need many of our humanistic qualities. The qualities of courage, forgiveness, inner strength, compassion, acceptance, vulnerability, and a willingness to resolve impeding aspects of the psyche, all need to be present. Then we can create the space and the possibility to allow the system to release its wounds, so that, as our hearts open a state of grace can unfold.

It is in this state of being, that we will find the truth of who we are. It is in being true to ourselves that we are then true to others. This may begin as surface work, but at some point it's about dropping below the surface, and examining the perhaps less than savoury or sweet aspects of ourselves, and our motivations for doing what we do or have done. This will place us in the optimum position should we wish to take personal responsibility for what is showing up in our world.

These simple questions are a good place to begin this part of the journey into being ourselves.

Why am I doing this?

What do I want or expect from this?

Why am I really doing this?

How does it make me feel to do this?

Is there anything I am avoiding feeling in myself by doing this?

A little self enquiry goes a long, long way. Stay aware and alert to any answers which contain, a "should, have to, must, ought to or supposed to" in them. Those answers are coming from the head, the desire to please others and fulfil external expectations. Any answers that contain an expectation, assumption or a what's in it for me factor, and other answers coming from the fear matrix, suck out any joy. Those answers are not heart centred

Whatever answers you give, be as honest and true as you can be with yourself. Then reassess, if you really want to do what you do, without the payoff? And I'm not just talking about survival and exchange for services, although at a deeper level they also come into play.

There are many gifted people who work in non governmental organisations (NGOs) around the world. Some are not as valued and respected as they could be, while some appear to be overvalued and respected. There are many reasons people work for NGOs and the work that is done is what keeps the human in humanitarian.

There are times when people will work for an NGO, seemingly coming from the heart, however, there is a "must, have to or should" attached to why they are doing what they do. On a subtle level, this may be masking guilt or masking their own pain, and this is therefore, a convenient transference onto a group. For example, someone who has experienced abuse in their lives and who then goes to work with war communities, without recognizing their own story, may at the same time be disassociating from their pain by focusing on a much bigger pain.

This is not to say that their work is not of value or needed, it is. Yet if they are able to acknowledge and work with their own pain, they would no longer be coming from a hidden agenda and their work would be energetically clean.

A human rights lawyer for example, does the work because they come from a privileged background and they feel they "should do" this for other less privileged people. A great thing to do, however, let's look at what's going on underneath.

I listened to the following reasoning from a human rights lawyer in East Timor in 2004. They felt that "by doing this I help others and I feel better about myself having had such a privileged upbringing." It felt like a justification and that what the person was really saying was 'I feel guilty, bad and/or ashamed about myself having had such a privileged background and this is a way I can get over it."

Imagine if that person could let go of their own self judgement and criticism. They could then work from the space of "I do this because it's what I do" or "I do this because I love it." The person would no longer be punishing themselves by working extreme hours, by never saying no, by having no limits and boundaries, and in the end running on empty for years and years. They would regain their own lives, and be better able to be of genuine service and assistance to others. Burnout would be less frequent, and a healthier environment would be created for all concerned.

I had conversations with such people in East Timor, as well as, in Cambodia, and those working in other parts of the world. I do support, respect and value the work such people do, often with few resources and little other support. It was an honour to witness the change that occurred in the health and well-being of people, when they moved out of their hidden agendas and transference patterns. The way in which they worked and the people that they worked for, changed. It changed to such a degree, that it transformed from a dependency relationship to an interdependent one, in a very short period of time. This was a shift from following the head, to following the heart and it benefited everyone in the equation.

I was personally motivated to go to college and to get a degree, because I wanted to prove to my parents that I could do it. In fact, when I look at my life with a more truthful eye, I see that much of what I did was to prove something to others.

The motivation did indeed get me to college. I got my BA honours degree, and I proved to others that I was "clever, capable and academic." I did not, however, check in with myself and see if I had proved something to myself, achieved something from my own eyes or how I felt about it from my own side.

That motivation led to the next challenge, and the next, and the next, always to prove something to others, so that maybe then they would love me. I was operating from low self-worth and was motivated from a sense of lack and fear. I calculated how I could get what I wanted. I was coming from the head and had little idea as to what following my heart was really all about.

The moment I decided to give notice from my teaching job in 2004, I stepped into following my heart. I have always wanted to make a difference in the world, to do things a different way, to live in greater unity, harmony and peace. I wanted this as a young child from a space of purity and innocence. Then as a teenager, I wanted to prove I was right and others were wrong. Now as an adult, a return to that innocence and purity of vision, has been allowed to resurface. This is now coupled with a willingness to just do it because I can and because it is there to be done.

If I had listened to my head, I never would have taken the months off to simply create, to honour my creative self, to paint and to write. As this book forms itself each morning, it is coming from the heart and the head, rather than the head alone. I have written this longhand so the head/heart connection can flow, and the balance of feminine and masculine, yin and yang, can blend and merge through paper and pen. I began writing for writings sake, for every time I started from "I should because," I dried up within a few hours or a few days. More experiential clarity I clearly needed.

You are the only person you need to prove anything to. You are the only one you need to do it for. You are the only one you need to love, to nurture and to be true to. As you can be true to you, the natural by-product is that you treat others better, and are real for others, present for others, loving and nurturing to others. When we are human towards ourselves, and allow our heart to guide us in harmony with our intuition and our head, we will be bringing our gifts to the fore, and those gifts are us.

To love ourselves as we do it, to nurture ourselves as we do it and to be true to ourselves as we do it, also means saying "no" when it might seem easier to say "yes"

Sixteen

Shame, Blame and Addictions

Shame leads to disengagement.

Blame leads to disconnection.

Addictions lead to isolation.

Shame is what keeps us on the outside of ourselves. Blame is what keeps us feeling like we are being kept on the outside by others. Addictions are what we use to stay on the outside of what we are really feeling.

I would say that at some point, nearly everyone has felt that feeling of being an "outsider." If we have all felt that, we are all the same, and that means, we are no longer an outsider.

Shame has stopped us from being ourselves, blame has prevented us from owning what is ours, and addictions have served to refill the wells of shame and blame, and numb the pain that we feel somewhere deep inside, of our disconnection from ourselves and others.

Shame stirs within us as a feeling, resulting from an action which then becomes a definition, such as "I am a mistake."

Guilt, in contrast arises in response to external judgements about an action, such as "I made a mistake."

Shame, is a challenge to acknowledge and move through. It is something to be felt and accepted. When we do, it transforms our very existence and frees us into being alive, and connected to ourselves and others.

Guilt is a signal to acknowledge something that we did. It is an opportunity to practice intelligent regret, to forgive ourselves and allow ourselves to be forgiven. When we do so, we can transform our future actions to create different outcomes.

Brene' Brown in her book *Daring Greatly*, writes at length about shame versus guilt, its impact on men and women, and the essential ingredient of vulnerability, to transform it. Reading her work and listening to her talks, can shift the way we view ourselves, the way we work and the way we relate to others.

Communities around the world, for the most part, although there are some exceptions amongst the indigenous tribes, employ shame to encourage moral behaviour and coerce people into acting or not acting in certain ways.

Morals change over time and they are different from ethics. Moral doctrines or rules have long been used to control others. Although the initial intention may have been a crystal clear one, they have been sullied over time as politicians, religious leaders, and others, have used moral arguments to boost their own standing and domination over others.

Morals are a viewpoint. Ethics, which are closely connected to moral conduct, are not about the abuse of power. They are about ways of behaving, such that the property and the state of another, comes to no harm. I see ethics as being secular, for everyone and for the highest good of all. I see morals as non-secular, religious and political, and frequently as having been manipulated to serve a few and restrict many.

Moral dogma is used to shame and blame, which supports the victim and abuser paradigms. It is principally coming from the fear matrix. The belief being that, unless we have these codes in place, people will run riot and control will be lost. I wonder how much moral dogma would be needed if abuse of money and status were taken out of the equation? What if the importance of money and status was diminished? Moral dogma adds to discrimination and separation. The use of moral dogma to stop or prevent the spread of the HIV virus, teenage pregnancy, polygamy and such like, has little to show for it, except that it has resulted in pushing such issues underground and increased the amount of deception in the world. It appears to have generated the phenomena of the saying "X denies any wrongdoing."

To shame another into acting a certain way is abuse, which may well backfire and extreme situations can unfold. Teenagers ridiculed by so-called friends or classmates in increasing numbers commit suicide. Others go on a killing spree to literally blast through the mantle of shame. In other cases the feeling of shame will pervade a person's relationship with themselves and with others, feeling a sense of low self-standing or self-esteem. In turn, this is then subtly perpetuated through media advertising campaigns, and the moral crusaders in the shape of politicians, and those behind those that govern.

Shame and blame appear to be bedfellows, lying on the sheets of humiliation. When we are shamed as a result of our action, we internalise it as a definition. "I am wrong, I am bad, I am a failure" and so on. We struggle with feelings of humiliation and do what we can to mask what we feel for fear that another may just pick up on it and expose us, resulting in more humiliation. The best way to avoid this is to deflect attention from ourselves, on to others. We frequently do this by blaming others for being the cause of whatever has gone "wrong, bad or failed."

According to Brene' Brown's work, shame is also gender specific. For women, to perceive themselves or be perceived as not being good enough or not perfect, is the fundamental trigger of shame, and for men, it is to perceive themselves to be or be perceived to be weak, that is their fundamental trigger of shame.

Whatever the triggers are, we all carry shame in our field. To date we generally do what we can to avoid it most of the time, by denying its existence. This denial leads to blaming others, when things happen that show us up. Fear of humiliation is what lies beneath.

Ritual humiliation in some cultures is a part of the transition from childhood to adulthood. However, when it was conducted by the elders, it was actually a ritual and a respectful honouring of a great moment in a person's life. Now however, we witness ritual humiliation in reality TV shows, in the media and in places of education, work and worship, as well as, in government. It does not seem to make for a more mature being and certainly not for a more mature audience. It does, however, serve to make many feel better about themselves, at the cost of the well-being of a few. The dance of abuser and victim continues for a few more songs.

Thus the rebel is born. Actually the rebel can arise for many reasons though shame, humiliation and blame are frequently part of its makeup. I smoked cigarettes for many years, though never before 06:00p.m, unless I'd been up all night and then that was a different story. I had given up a few times, like when I went trekking in Nepal and it took little effort to do so. However, I took up smoking as soon as I returned to Jakarta. Looking back at it, it was a way to annoy my parents, a way to assert my independence, and a way to be different, and ironically to fit into the "scene" as one of the cool people.

This last reason started to touch on the real reason I smoked. When I uncovered it, I dropped all desire for cigarettes in a snap. I have heard hypnotherapists say that smoking is directly linked to low self-esteem, and I know in my case that was true. I mean apart from liking cigarettes, and being addicted to the chemicals, why would you put carbon monoxide into your lungs along with a few other noxious chemicals if you actually loved, liked or valued yourself?

At a new school for my last two years, before going on to college, I was telling a story to some new friends. As I spoke, I used my hands, gesticulating to add feeling to what I was saying. That was normal for me, yet it appeared unusual for one of these new friends, who took my hands and arms and held them behind my back and said "now keep telling your story." They took my hands and the story continued to unfold. Everyone laughed, myself included, to hide my embarrassment, and at a deeper level, mask my sense of shame at being so noticeably different.

I had not yet begun to appreciate that being different could also be seen as a gift.

Not long afterwards I began to smoke properly, and I realise with hindsight, that it was the perfect way to deflect attention away from what I was doing with my hands when talking. As a smoker, there is a lighter, a box of matches, or a cigarette in one or both of our hands. They can be in constant motion and no one will make a comment about it. To hide my shame, I became a smoker and then a drinker.

My smoking was clearly linked to embarrassment, a lesser form of shame perhaps. After having experienced Bert Hellinger's work of the *Movement of the Soul* or better known *Family Constellation*, I know that the shame of not fitting in was triggered down the ancestral line. Some of my ancestors were Armenian and they had fled Armenia during the troubles with Turkey and ended up as refugees in the UK.

My addiction to fitting in and being a rebel at the same time, took me to some very different and out of the way places, and altered states of being. I never truly became physically addicted to anything, and I realise I was incredibly lucky. I definitely developed a habit of altering my sate of being when I went out clubbing, yet when I decided to stop I had no cravings or withdrawls. The rebel, as it turns out, is closely connected to victim identity. In contrast to "poor me" it has more of an asserted "look at me" approach.

I appreciate that I have been extraordinarily blessed and watched over on many levels by a much higher consciousness than my "self" at that time, which was a rather destructive one. For some of us, there is a celebration in coming out the other side, unscathed yet having learnt a lot and being healthy. For others there is a lengthy and at times lifelong struggle with addiction, that becomes so physical, that it appears to override the conscious, subconscious, and mental and emotional issues of shame. There but for the grace of All That Is, go I.

Alcohol and other substances were ways that I tried to sabotage myself, even if I said "it is for fun and recreation." When it becomes a regular past time, it is no longer for recreation, it is actually to kill the pain, kill the shame and to kill ourselves.

The most debilitating addiction I did have, which took me longer to stop, was the disease to please. It was that addiction that led me to all the patterns of abuse. I stay aware of it to this day, so that I can catch it if, and when, it resurfaces.

It took me a long time to realise that the person I was hurting the most, with my rebel's habits was myself, and that if I was to continue on with them, then the biggest hurt would still be happening to me. I was in fact, increasing my own sense of shame, and blaming it on life on the planet being too hard. I was ashamed to be human in fact. As I woke up to this, I looked around at the ways I was attempting to check out of life through my addictions. I looked at nature, it seemed to accept itself, it seemed to accept me, no comparisons there and a switch began.

I had been given this precious life and although I had played with not wanting it, through my patterns and habits, I actually loved life and wanted to be fully in it. That meant cleaning up and for me it was about cleaning up the mental and emotional issues, which allowed the physical to drop its superficial addictions, as it turned out, and for other aspects to awaken.

Addictions are not just about drugs, pharmaceuticals or recreationals, tobacco and alcohol. Addictions show up in so many forms and it's worth looking at how they serve us and how they impede us.

We are all addicts. We all have an addictive gene. It just depends how it is activated as to whether our addictions are more or less socially acceptable. The sooner we realise and accept that we are all addicts, be it to patterns of thought, drugs, behaviour or material goods, the sooner we can begin to address the impeding aspects of the addictive gene as a collective, and switch to the helpful qualities.

Drug addiction is an illness, and once we start to treat it as such, we may then be able to be of greater assistance to those who are living with drug addiction every day. Our judgements keep people stuck in a place that is not helpful. We all need to review how we perceive each other, as well as, ourselves. It is the only way we will change anything, and until we are really willing to take a holistic approach and look at the social causes, we are burying our heads in the sand, and condemning others to a life of constant struggle and debilitating addictions.

People become addicted to TV shows, to foods, to ways of thinking, to depression and other emotions. People become addicted to other people, to sugar, to drinks, to brands and labels, to gadgets, to their roles, to gambling, to being who they think they should be and to their created identity. People become addicted to the computer, the smart phone, social media, messaging services, addicted to fear and pessimism, addicted to romantic love, to fast cars, addicted to fantasies, addicted to cosmetic surgery, to tattoos, and piercings. Whatever it is, an addiction will consume most of your wakened energy and may even show up in your sleep too.

Addictions take us out of the present experience. We are either, planning how we can get more and thinking about what it will be like when we have it, or we are reflecting on what it was like when we had it. If our so called harmless addictions take us out of the heart and into the head, and take us out of the present and out of feel, perhaps they are not so harmless after all. We will have disconnected from our compassionate essence selves, and entered ever more deeply into a cycle of pain and suffering as a result.

If we are not covering over, or numbing an underlying sense of shame, and are trying to subconsciously fit in or punish ourselves, the ability to drop the addiction happens in an instant. Even though there may be physical hardship to follow, the mental and emotional breakthroughs assist us to start caring enough about ourselves, to find the best way for us to address the physical aspects.

Addressing the personal issue of shame, from a space of forgiveness, one step at a time, is a good place to start. The idea is to diminish the shame felt, rather than to compound it further through self-criticism and blame.

Some patterns or habits take a while to dissolve, shake off or let go of and it is wise to take it one day at a time. If needed, it is important to find good therapists and an appropriate modality or group that can support and encourage us, to move through and out of the identity we used to be. There are many to choose from and some of the oldest like Alcoholics Anonymous (AA) or Narcotics Anonymous (NA), really are tried and tested and work very well for many. They do not suit everyone however, so look around and find what is going to work for you. We need to create space so that we can gradually emerge into what we would prefer to be, where we would prefer to be, and how we would prefer to be. It is a journey in itself and we do deserve all the support that is waiting to be received.

For some stopping cosmetic surgery is as challenging as stopping recreational or pharmaceutical drugs. Both share a common root, that of not being enough, somewhere along the line. It is an insidious collective consciousness belief, and one we can make contributions to change.

When we decide to address our particular addiction by trying to "give it up," observing where our attention is most of the time, will be very helpful. If we decide to address our particular addiction by "stopping it," observing where our attention is most of the time, will be liberating.

When we give something up, it can often feel as if we are depriving ourselves of something and therefore our attention, subconsciously or consciously, is always going back to the thing that we are trying to give up.

In contrast however, when we stop something, it is done. Our attention is then free to move on to something else. The choice between giving up and stopping is worth making deliberately.

To be consciously aware of what we are actually undertaking, is a gift, for it affects the energetic of what unfolds next.

As we change we may or may not return to our past habit, just to "see" if we are over it. If we do and it's still a life or death reaction, we clearly aren't free from it. Stop it. There is more work to be done on the inner realms. If we feel we can dip in and out, it is time to be mindful of our own ability to deceive ourselves. If we are in neutral, there is no need to even check in on ourselves, as life will be presenting other things for us to put our attention on.

At some point, the world appears to be more expansive than it was before, there are more things to do in our community than we realised before and our friendships often feel more meaningful as well.

When we can be true to ourselves there is no longer any need to say yes, when we would rather say no. Likewise there is no need to say no when we really want to say yes. Shame will keep us in a holding position, just like guilt. Blame will also keep us locked up and seeing the world as out to get us, rather than appreciating that it is coming from us. It's time we stepped up to our personal responsibility and became actively involved in the creation of that world.

The following questions may assist in that process. Take some time to ask yourself and contemplate the answers that come.

What am I withholding from myself?

What am I not allowing myself to receive?

Who am I trying to punish or take revenge on?

Who, do I believe, did not give me what I am now denying myself?

Who, do I believe, did not meet my expectation of how it should have been, in what I now deny myself?

Feel where it sits in the body.

Allow yourself to slip quietly into the subconscious mind and the thing you deny yourself will arise along with the person or people you are attempting to punish. Start by dropping out of the head and falling into the heart.

Do the forgiveness process and reclaim your heart as well - if necessary.

For example and this was one of mine; denying myself love to avenge those I felt didn't give it to me or didn't give me enough of it. Bizarrely we try to punish them by denying ourselves what we believe we didn't receive from others, and by playing the victim. The interesting thing about the victim identity is that it will eventually kill us unless we dissolve it. That is true of the rebel as well. Its psychological make up is designed to keep us as a victim. We will perpetually create dramas where we end up being victimised either by another person, life events or circumstances. We are punishing ourselves, masquerading as a victim, yet actually being an abuser of others. We are wallowing in the fear of lack, and projecting it on to others.

When I came out of a long relationship I was sitting in shame. I realised this with hindsight, rather than at the time. I was ashamed and believed I had failed as a woman because the relationship had failed. I gradually disengaged from relationships to hide my shame. As I disengaged, I blamed myself, my ex-partner and even the place where I was living. I became addicted to numbing the pain by going out most nights. I was isolating myself from the pain, and isolating myself from the people and the world around me.

It was through using the techniques above that I was able to move through this layer with grace, gentleness and ease and come into more of being myself.

As we begin to recognize and acknowledge this, we can begin to emerge from hurt ego to healthy essence.

Seventeen

Relationships

We live in a vibrational universe. We are energy. Everything is pure energy and energies interact. They attract and repulse. They are constantly moving even when in their most solid forms and as, so called, inert matter. Stuck energy is not, not moving it is simply contained and vibrating within its container. If there is sufficient pressure there will be an implosion or an explosion and that will create some space for a bit more free movement. A relationship between two people can be very much the same.

There are as many types of relationships as there are lovers and partners in the world. Each has unique characteristics and is a reflection of the two or more people interacting at any given moment. We are also coming to the relationship with imprints from our parents, family of origin, ancestors and society, so frequently there are more energies present, than the people in the relationship. The work of Claude Steiner, *Scripts People Live*, sheds a lot of light on this aspect.

There are many supportive, loving, evolving relationships, though we do not hear much about them. They tend to be given less air time. There are many relationships which are undermining, destructive and imploding or exploding and these are the ones that seem to receive the air time. It would appear that we are addicted to drama and sending subliminal messages to collective consciousness that this is just how relationships are. It feels timely to bring our attention to what elements may contribute to a relationship of interdependence and a relationship of equals. In order to do that however, examining our current state is invaluable.

Firstly it may be helpful to look at some terms, codependent, dependent, interdependent and independent. Codependent and independent are at the opposite ends to the spectrum and the fear matrix seems to play out in both of them. In codependent, there is a fear of being left. In independent there is a fear of being trapped. Dependent and interdependent meet in the middle and are an honest acknowledgement of where we are, as beings on the planet, in relation to each other and all things. The differences between them are slight.

In my view, dependency recognizes the importance of others in our lives and our need for connection. When this is balanced, all is well. Yet there may be times when one person feels more dependent than the other, so there are possibilities for subtle levels of fear to arise, usually around fear of the future if the other was to leave.

Interdependency recognizes that this is a symbiotic relationship, where both parties are interconnected and dependent on each other, while at the same time being separate beings.

I may be splitting hairs here, however an interdependent relationship is what forms the foundation for a relationship of equals.

I have long believed that there are three constancies in life. One is change, the other is you, and that you is constantly changing. The third is breath. If we bear this in mind, regarding relationships, the pit falls which we tend to fall into, largely as a result of expectations and assumptions, become suddenly more obvious and as such, are much more easily avoided.

Another belief I have held is that it is possible to have a relationship of equals and I have looked to my god parents as a model of such a relationship. I know their relationship had its challenges along the way, yet their manner of relating with each other was as equals, and it was a pleasure to behold and a joy to be around them.

I have been told, on a number of occasions that this vision that I hold true to my heart, of a relationship of equals, and one that is interdependent, is simply a fantasy and does not and cannot exist. I feel a deep sadness when I hear such things, for it is as if all remembrance of who we be, has gone and that people are settling for what they can get, rather than allowing themselves and others to be all that they can be.

Definitions may be helpful here for clarity and ease of expression regarding a relationship of equals. Equal does not mean that within a relationship, all involved must be earning the same amount of income. That they must be working the exact same hours and, or that they must be sharing the daily chores. All those as factors have an impact on the relationship, but they are not what I mean by a relationship of equals.

For me, a relationship of equals is one where the beings are able to meet themselves and each other exactly where they are, as they are. It means that they continue to allow themselves and the other to do what energy does, that is be in motion. An interdependent relationship of equals means to be willing to allow the relationship to take its own course, and to be guardians of the sacredness of the union of love.

This requires courage. It requires self standing or self-esteem. It requires being in integrity with ourselves and with the other. It is about honour and respect. Relationships are not a giving up. They are a growing with, a growing towards and a growing into. A relationship is an opportunity to experience a symbiotic relationship, just like in nature, where the tree is in a symbiotic relationship with the earth, and with everything on the planet, including humans. We seem to have forgotten this however, in the paradigm of humans' domination over everything else.

A tree not only feeds from the earth but it feeds the earth in return. As it draws nutrients up from its roots in the soil, it also binds that soil and creates the appearance of stability upon which, we as humans build. The tree, through its leaves, gives back nutrients to the soil and to the earth, sustaining not only itself, but also the myriad of life forms found within the soil, and within its own structure.

The tree also draws in, inhales, Carbon dioxide, CO_2, from the atmosphere via its leaves, and then converts that CO_2, exhaling Oxygen, O_2, which sustains not only the tree and other flora but also all the fauna, including humans. Anything that needs O_2 to live, is reliant on the symbiotic relationship that this tree is creating. Nature enables us to sustain life. Why, I wonder, are we as a collective still so intent on destroying that which sustains our lives? Suicidal tendencies, it appears, are running high in the collective consciousness.

An interdependent relationship of equals is just like the tree and the earth. This is not about the earth being better or more important that the tree, or the tree being better or more important than the earth. It is that they feed and sustain each other's existence. One in competition with the other is self defeating and self destructive. The same happens to us when we are operating from the matrix of fear.

When we stay or remain in situations at work, which we are no longer aligned with, it is time to move on, and let another step into their right place and us into ours. In a marriage or partnership I hear people struggle with staying together for the children's sake. Children know if their parents are not happy. It is a disservice to the children, to stay together unhappily. Separate, reorganise and renegotiate the relationship, so that the children get to enjoy the best of both of people, and in turn we get to transform into being the best we can be, without pretence.

If we stay together for the children, as magnanimous as that gesture may appear to be on the surface, it is filled with dishonesty and betrayal. We are lying to ourselves and possibly using our children to hide from our own fear of being alone, of not finding another and so forth. The mechanics of fear are like a magnet. We draw to us that which we fear, through our very refusal to look at it head on and feel it.

Face that fear, stop hiding behind the children, sooner or later we will manifest and experience that fear, and we will find ourselves alone. Better to be with it as it arises, than to let it grow ever bigger and more overwhelming. Staying together for the children can mean there is an unspoken semi or subconscious resentment towards the children for keeping us in a situation, that part of us would rather no longer be in. Children feel it. Our partner feels it. Our friends will feel it. It is a lie, and it is betraying ourselves and what we know to be right for us.

This is not advocating jumping out of a challenging relationship and into our fantasies. Put in the time, the effort and the sincere motivation to address the challenges. Seek out the many professionals who can guide and give support through the challenges, and do the work on ourselves as individuals. Take responsibility for our "stuff" and stop blaming our partner or spouse. Handle what is ours and create space, so that our partner, if willing to do so, can address theirs. Then, just perhaps, the relationship can transform from challenging to enjoyable, healthy and loving, together or apart.

Commit to yourself and then you can commit to others. Take the responsibility off the children, and allow self honesty, integrity, respect and honour to permeate all relationships. This includes the one we have with ourselves, out to the ones we have with others. Krishnamurti in his book *Freedom from the Known* also gives wonderful insights and practices for living with ourselves, as we are and for being in relationships.

Commitment is rich with connotations. We make committments at a time when they are right for us, as the being that we are, at that time. Then we believe that commitment is fixed. Ironic, when everything else is changing. Perhaps if we were to reframe commitment and see it as constant yet fluid, we would become better at honouring the ones we make. Perhaps, then we would be able and willing to review and renegotiate our commitments, in order to continue to be in alignment with them and who we are now. We would then be in integrity, and in a position to truly honour commitments to the self and others.

Communication is the key to any authentic relationship, no matter what kind of relationship it is. Family relationships, a marriage, a partnership, a friendship and so forth, all require respectful authentic communication. The works of John M Gottman, PhD, *The Marriage Clinic* and *The Science of Trust*, along with Claude Steiner's *Scripts People Live*, and Gary Chapman's *The 5 Love Languages*, are valuable in different ways, for their insights and impact on relating in relationships,

The matrix of love, just to remind ourselves, is based on trust, allowing and acceptance and it creates space, freedom and peace. It is also about unity, harmony, interdependence and balance. The matrix of fear is based on hope, control and limitations and it creates contractions, restrictions, pain and suffering. It also creates separation, codependency, conflict and imbalance.

Ask yourself what kind of relationship matrix would you prefer to be in, in your world?

Given the choice I am sure most would choose the former rather than the latter. This begs yet another question of course. What type of person do we need to be in order to attract or create such a relationship in our lives?

Interestingly, it is ourselves we actually need to be trusting of, allowing and accepting of. We need to be enjoying and radiating space, freedom and peace. We will attract what we are emanating. When we are being hopeful, controlling, limiting, contracting, and restrictive towards ourselves, we will be emanating pain and suffering. If like attracts like, and we know that it does, this is exactly what we will draw into our world.

We fear that which we really, really, really want.

We fear that it will happen and then what?

We attract that which we fear.

We sabotage out of fear that which we really want, believing we are not good enough or deserving of it.

We fear that if we get what we really want, we'll lose it somehow. Perhaps it will be taken from us or it will disappear.

We grasp onto that which we have, wanting it to stay the same forever, in a world where everything and everyone is constantly changing. We set ourselves up for disappointment before we even get off the ground.

We hold such unexpressed desires, expectations and assumptions within ourselves, out of fear that if we express them, they'd go unmet, be seen as unreasonable, or be unheard. At the same time we project those unvoiced expectations, beliefs, desires and assumptions onto the other, and we cannot fathom why they do not meet them. Once more the disappointment grows into the excuses, subtle anger and resentment, which over time grows into withdrawal and silent rage, sitting between the beings in the space of relationship.

If we are unwilling to be accepting, loving, trusting and supportive of ourselves, allowing ourselves, all the space and freedom we need, to express the multifaceted being that we are, if we refuse ourselves peace, how can we even begin to offer it to another, let alone receive it fully from another?

To create an interdependent relationship of equals, where the relationship is recognised as a coalescence of energies from the parties involved, requires courage. Courage to continue to be who we be, and to allow the other to be who they be. Kahlil Gibran in *The Prophet* expresses it wonderfully in his verses *On Marriage*, verse three of which I quote here.

> *Give your hearts, but not into each other's keeping,*
> *For only the hand of Life can contain your hearts.*
> *And stand together yet not too near together:*
> *For the pillars of the temple stand apart,*
> *And the oak tree and the cypress grow not in each*
> *other's shadow.*
> (Gibran 1999, verse III p24)

Unless we are willing to do the work on ourselves, to take time to be still, to reflect, to be mindful, and to allow consciousness to become more aware of itself as existence, we shall continue to create the codependent and impeding, harmful, dysfunctional, destructive relationships, we currently experience and view in the world.

It is time to clean up our own back yard, weed the garden and to make ready the land. For love knows no boundaries. Love knows no conditions. Love has no limitations.

Within a relationship, the mutual recognition of the preciousness of the gift of love, leads to a commitment, to strive to be the best custodians and guardians of love that each being can be.

The games that are played, the damage that is done, the dreams that are shattered and the hearts that are broken, by our unwillingness to be our authentic selves, to discover who we are, to recover and reclaim the various parts of ourselves which we have disowned, means we perpetuate the cycle of pain and suffering for ourselves, each other and the future others.

To address it as the games are played and the heart breaks, is to take up the opportunity presented by such critical and challenging moments. These moments are those where we can start to become ourselves. Moments where we can start to become more authentic and real with ourselves and therefore with others. To take time and be still with the shattered dreams, to reflect on what was our contribution to the unravelling of the relationship, to look at how we could have been a better custodian of love, will benefit ourselves and others immensely.

Divorce, death or separation can bring with it the urge to dive into another relationship. It is a good idea to try leaving all the baggage behind, otherwise we will be taking the past with us, projecting it on to the present and creating a future we have already experienced in the past!

The urge to escape the pain can be intense and yet what happens is the pain gets buried deep within, only to surface at some later time in some unrelated situation or in the physical body. The pain does not disappear just because we have checked out. We have disappeared and when we decide to come back and be in our lives, we will find the pain is still there waiting for us. To acknowledge it, to be with it, means it can then diminish and start to dissolve. This frees up the space for us to fill it and be filled up with our very essence, and that essence is Love.

The more we run from ourselves, from our own creations, our shame, expectations, assumptions and pain, the more we will avoid being present, and the more we will be susceptible to operating less consciously and deliberately through the matrix of fear. We are inviting the victim and abuser to remain part of our ruling psyche, and victims joining together, play out a whole new cycle of the victim - abuser - victim game. Expectations and assumptions are part of this game and worthy of more exploration.

It is time for us to choose to create relationships which are coming from the matrix of love, so that they can be sustaining, healthy, vibrant and life giving.

Eighteen

Expectations and Assumptions - Happiness is an Inside Job

Expectations are a wonderful illustration of how we get in our own way, take ourselves out of the present, and set ourselves up for disappointment, miscommunication, and frequently a fair amount of pain and suffering. Expectations are based on hope rather than on actuality. Hope is an aspect of the fear matrix.

Assumptions are when we accept or perhaps it would be more accurate to say, when we project something to be a certain way, without any proof that it is, in fact, that way. Assumptions are what we think another is thinking or feeling or planning, and we do not even ask them if this is in fact the case. We are creating a story in our own head and controlling the script. Control is an aspect of the fear matrix.

Expectations and assumptions impinge on most aspects of our lives, to varying degrees and with varying impact. Expectations and assumptions are our own version of what or how we would like things to happen, someone to be, the world to unfold and so forth. Expectations and assumptions are linked to the matrix of fear. They are our bid at controlling the flow of energy, and they create a disconnection from the experience of what is actually happening and what we would like to be happening.

We seem to experience neither fully and the one we do experience, we go into resistance with, because it's not the one we desire or want to experience. So we are locked in the loop of resistance and desire. We are absolutely stuck until we can see the expectation, that is to say, belief, that we are operating through and accept exactly where we are right here, right now.

Relationships are fertile land for expectations to express themselves in disappointment and falling out. There is a wonderful saying "do as you would be done by", taken from the character of the same name 'Mrs Do-as-you-would-be-done-by' in Charles Kingsley's *The Water Babies*. This is an echo of the edicts of many religions "treat a neighbour as thyself," "treat others as you would like to be treated" and so on. This is a great instruction, as long as, one can dissolve the expectation that may arise with it.

When I treated someone how I would like to be treated, I used to expect them to treat me as I had treated them. I assumed everyone knew this was the payback for being nice. When they appeared not to do that, I would get upset, annoyed and feel let down. That set up a run of harmful thoughts, and my world would shrink and become a place of pain and suffering, conflict and disappointment. On a personal integrity level, it showed I was operating from a hidden agenda of "be nice so others will be nice to me," rather than being authentic.

The person we have treated so well, may not be the person who treats us well. It is worth while dropping that expectation, doing so will create more space in all our relationships. In this life time we may have treated them well, yet if we're open to the concept of reincarnation, we may appreciate that in a past lifetime, we may well have treated them, or another, rather poorly and this is now showing up in our world.

Another expectation is that because it has been easy for us to meet and fulfil another's needs, from our own perspective, that that same person will automatically be able and willing, to meet and fulfil ours. We even assume that they will want to do this and will know intuitively when we will need them to do so. This can be crushing within relationships and just like the example above, it is mistaken and untrue. To expect and assume our beloved will meet all our expectations and assumptions, and fulfil all our needs, is codependency. It is part of the same illusion of giving them our heart and making another responsible for our life, happiness, evolution and livelihood. Happiness is an inside job.

As people, we tend to have a variety of friends. Some we go out dancing with, others we have long conversations with, others coffee, some we go on holiday with, yet others on a retreat, others on long walks, on shopping sprees, and with some we may do absolutely nothing with, which feels really good. We do not look to one friend to fulfil all the needs of our multidimensional or multifaceted personality, so why are we putting it all onto our beloved?

At some point in a relationship, expectations start to take over and play out. Many are found in collective consciousness and supported on a more subliminal level, via the films we watch, the advertisements we view and the magazines we read. Expectations change over time. With new generations, new perspectives and viewpoints are expressed. There do however, still seem to be some archetypal patterns and these expectations, operating within our psyches, are often below the radar of our conscious awareness. They deserve examination.

There are many different ways to become more conscious and aware of the expectations and assumptions we are operating through, so do not feel limited to just one method. I have used observation, as well as, kinesiology, NAET clearing, homoeopathy, dream analysis, the morning pages, long walks on the beach, silent retreats, as well as, going out and dancing and lying in a hot bath and chanting for half an hour.

Whatever it takes, whatever works, do it. Sometimes a card reading will help to illuminate areas of confusion and shadow, so that we can get the clarity we need to move once more. It's got to be better than festering in a pit of anger, resentment, disappointment, pain and suffering. I have found that in using various modalities, either singularly or combined, that I am able to integrate the diverse angles within one expectation. A conversation with another can also bring Aha's. When we are open to seeing our teacher in everyone and everything, it is amazing how quickly we will recover the answers that have been lying quietly within.

A classic example, I own this is all from my own side, occurred between a boyfriend and I. I felt I had supported my boyfriend to get his new career off the ground, doing whatever I could to make sure that he was successful. I was playing out a childhood pattern where his success was down to me, by making myself not good enough. A few months down the track I got the second part of that pattern, like a slap across the face. I had an art exhibition and needed some help to hang the paintings. I asked the aforementioned boyfriend for help and was told "sorry I can't, I'm too busy".

Incredulous, I then became furious. Thoughts of "after everything I've done for him and he couldn't, wouldn't, wasn't able to help me for one day!" ran through my mind. The anger turned to resentment and I buried the disappointment as far as I could, deep inside. I felt that he could have changed the dates of the catalogue shoot if he had wanted to help me, but he didn't. I assumed he didn't care. I went silent, fearful of what might happen if I expressed my anger and disappointment.

In the end it was a friend of his who helped me, and this friend was one I didn't particularly like. He would take my boyfriend out on a big night out that would last most of the weekend. Ironic indeed, that it was the one person I viewed, as being out to sabotage our relationship, who stepped in to help me. An example of how treating others as we would like to be treated, may come back to us through someone other than the person we have been treating so nicely.

The relationship continued to deteriorate. My unspoken anger and resentment were ever present in the field, and the sadness and disappointment I felt was permeating the world I was viewing.

Not once did I verbally share with my partner how I felt about his response. I let it fester deep within.

I expected my beloved to work out why I was so withdrawn. I expected him to understand why I felt as I felt. I expected him to make amends. All without me saying a word, without me expressing what was happening on my inner realms and without me asking for assistance, let alone even asking the question why, so that I could better understand the full picture. So I wallowed and when we did put the relationship to rest, all that sadness finally came out and I grieved for long time.

Eventually I realised I was grieving for the me that I had put second, the me I had sidelined, and the me I had let down. All this I projected on to him, yet it was me that was operating through the beliefs, *I'm not good enough* and *I do not deserve to express my feelings.*

The gift of hindsight gave me much more of an overview. As a professional, appointments do not just get cancelled, unless there is an emergency. Our dates clashed and a friend stepped in to help, probably because they had been asked to, but that was something I had been way too grumpy to find out about.

An expectation is also something of a hidden agenda. If we really want to get down to cleaning up what may be going on, on a very subtle level, we need to look at this.

If I treat someone fairly and am generous with my time, believing I am doing so because I can and because I wish to be, when they then treat me by being stingy and ungrateful, and I react with anger and resentment at this behaviour, it this is a sure sign that I have been operating through an expectation of being treated in the same way.

I will first look at the expectation and then I will ask myself, "if I had not had that expectation running would I have actually given all that I did in the first place?"

If the answer is no, then I have found my subtle, but very real hidden agenda. I am operating through, *if I am nice to you, you will be nice to me.* My action is conditional and fear based. The realisation that most of my life had been conducted through a hidden agenda, happened in January 2004 and was quite a show stopper for me. Since then I have repeatedly asked myself the questions

Do I really want to do this?

Do I expect anything back?

I then address the answer as best I am able to do so at the time.

To be in a relationship and express unconditional love really is a great thing to aspire to. If however, we could just accept where we are today, and be more open and transparent to ourselves and in our interactions with others, that would already make a big difference. It may seem such a big thing, yet if we approach all our relations, friendships, acquaintances, family and lovers in this way, we can start, step by step, to become more genuine in our dealings and more authentic in our interactions. This affects the work that we do, as well as, the way we move in the world.

To do something simply because we do and we be, is to be coming from a space of purity of heart, a rare attribute in most communities and societies in the world. However, that doesn't mean it's impossible. We can each start from where we are right now, to be more honest in our dealings and more transparent in our actions. There is a freedom that unfolds when hidden agendas are owned. As integrity is restored, energy flows and grace arises within interactions. Where once animosity or a low level of mistrust walked alongside the principal players on the stage of life, there is now a willingness to be in authentic communion with each other.

My expectation not being met, led to the assumption that my partner didn't care and that led to me withholding my love and my thoughts from him and eventually saw the demise of the relationship. Expectations and assumptions often go hand in hand. For example, I had once asked for flowers wanting romantic gestures to be more present in our relationship. The man went out and brought me an orchid saying "now I never have to buy you flowers again." This did not meet my expectation of having flowers every week. I assumed he didn't really care or understand what I meant, and that he was lazy.

In fact, an orchid keeps right on flowering, given the right conditions and can last a lifetime. If I had taken it that way, his action could have been an incredible declaration and expression of romantic love. I missed it as such at the time, for my expectations were in the way. They acted as a filter to block what I was actually experiencing. That romantic love expectation came from watching films, TV shows, reading love stories and so forth. I was creating a story in my mind, projecting it onto him and then reproaching him for not fulfilling a dream I assumed he also held. My assumption was in the way. That dream wasn't even stemming from having consciously examined desires, let alone the ones we expressed to each other.

It is all part of the spiral of life and just because I can now see those expectations and assumptions, doesn't mean that they have all fallen away from my life. I too am a work in progress. It does, however, mean I can catch things more easily if or when they appear, which is a gift.

The subconscious is deep and multilayered, so I am aware and alert to further revelations and opportunities to become freer, more genuine, more transparent and authentic in my dealings with myself and others. It can be fun, if I make it so, once I have grasped that the anger and disappointment is coming from me and my dear expectations.

Expectations and assumptions are the mother and father of misunderstandings and their grandparents, fear of loss and hope, all come from the matrix of fear. They are the source of our pain and suffering.

As a final word, expectations and assumptions also impact upon our experiences of things. If we have a friend who raves about a therapist, a treatment or a place and we go expecting the same experience, we are assuming that we share the same taste as our friend. We had better be prepared for disappointment. We will not be allowing ourselves to experience what is actually happening to us and we will be looking out for and comparing it to someone else's experience. Their experience is theirs not ours. We are we and they are they, as far as an experience is concerned. Some people love one country but others hate it. We can by all means go and find out for ourselves. Perhaps have some useful facts, but then drop all expectations and assumptions, and go with an open mind so that we can be in the moment and receive whatever experience is there waiting for us.

To truly experience our life, we need to do exactly the same.

Nineteen
Life is an Offering -
Love the Body, Love the Planet

The body is our primary vehicle of expression in this life time and it is through it, that we can become more aware of ourselves. We have been gifted a body through which to experience this existence on the planet. I am referring to our spirit, the essence of us and the pure awareness aspect of ourselves. If we wish to be ourselves, it makes sense to connect more deeply with our body and become more aware of what we are putting into it, and even whether we are actually in it.

There are people who experience "space" within the body. Astronauts and pilots have been stretching out to the limits of space supported by current technology. Most of us however, are experiencing our lives through the physical structure of the body.

Pure awareness is however limitless. It is as infinite as the space in which we live, the universe and the galaxies. When having the privilege to watch a newly born baby or animal, notice how they move around as if experimenting with this new form. They are still in a state of remembering that they are more than just a form. After a few months, the greater density of form begins to manifest, and the awareness of being more than form begins to diminish.

In Bali, it is believed that after six weeks the child has begun to let go of its cosmic origins and by six months it is landing on the Earth. For those of the royal cast, they are often held above the earth for up to one year. There is a ceremony to mark the arrival on Earth and it affirms the embodiment of the body by the spirit. This spirit is remembered and recognised as an intrinsic part of life in the Balinese culture.

This understanding is not limited to the portals of birth and death. Should an accident occur, a ceremony will be conducted to recall the spirit back to the body. It is understood that when accidents or traumatic events occur, our spirit will "check out" of the body and that it is important to call it back in. This knowledge and technique is also understood by secular shamans, healers and therapists the world over.

Past life regression or soul retrieval aims to do the same thing, at times stretching back into previous incarnations where there may have been a violent death. It is, in a manner of speaking, possible to experience oneself as being other than the body.

The realisation and clarity that arises when we appreciate, on an experiential level, that we are more than the body, is something beyond wondrous. We can experience an overwhelming feeling of a homecoming; a remembrance and an innate sense of knowingness. That sensation and connection can be extraordinarily and intensely familiar. It is as if one is touching everything, indeed there is an All That Is feeling. Standing still in the presence of the natural world, can evoke such a feeling. Spend any time with Whales, and feel the vastness of everything merge into everything.

The body however, is what we are in and we are blessed to function and express ourselves through it. It is an incredible gift. It has been studied by scientists, medical doctors and ourselves to different depths, for eons and yet still its mysteries elude us. Interestingly that as with nature, there are those areas which we believe we can control, repair or fix and we are able to do so. There are others however, where the interferences cause more complications, and even poison the system through the use of strong chemical cocktails.

Our dis-ease manifests through the physical and the nervous system. The foods, liquids and substances we put into and on our bodies do have an effect. As we have seen, thoughts can also be toxic. There are so many books, articles and research papers about "you are what you eat." Complimentary medicine recognizes the impact of diet. Ayurvedic and Chinese medicine both view diet, as an intrinsic part of the diagnostic process.

I find it interesting that current allopathic or Western medicine, rarely enquires about the dietary input of the patient. I find this even more interesting given the number of additives in processed foods and the general rise in conditions of health, which are directly related to what we are consuming every day. Diabetes II and obesity both spring to mind. There is also the rise in the sensitivity of the system and allergic reactions experienced by so many adults and children alike.

A change in diet can alter a person's physical state of dis-ease. This in the long term could mean a redirection of funding in health services, towards preventative care rather than for day and aftercare.

The body, like the planet is largely made up of water and yet we are facing a clean water crisis in many parts of the world. Water is being taken out of the wells and springs, where it is freely available to everyone, and then it is sold back to people depleted of its natural minerals. In most cases, it is sold in plastic bottle bottles, at incredibly inflated prices and with the possibility of ingesting PCBs and other chemicals.

The Sixth Wave, by James Bradfield Moody and Bianca Nogrady, is a well researched and ethical book that looks at the environmental impact of many industries upon the planet. For example, to make a plastic bottle requires three times as much water as the bottle actually contains. The petrochemical industry, of which plastic is a by-product, pollute the water systems along with other industries every single day.

We ourselves pollute rivers and waterways every single day, through our use of detergents, perfumes, the clothes we wear, the medications we take and so forth. Ironically the same toxins that we put into our bodies, through being unaware, are the same ones we are putting into our waterways, through choosing to remain ignorant.

The outer world and the environment is a reflection of our inner world and environment. With all the knowledge and know-how that we have and have access to, why is it that we choose to stay in an ignorant state and continue to make ourselves and our environment toxic? Why do we then play out the victim, when we become aware that we have the physical manifestation of disease?

The world in which we live is a dynamic and fascinating place. Creation itself is extraordinary and technology equally so. Somewhere along the way, when the two are out of sync with each other, misalignment occurs. Indeed for humanity and nature at this current time, the conflict appears to be intensifying. "*When the external technology matches the internal knowledge and vice versa, when the external knowledge matches the internal technology then we have the ascension to the new world.*" (Haramein 2003)

When they are misaligned we have disaster. The polluted state of the waterways and oceans, the fallout from nuclear power plants and gas companies' fracking, are examples. They too however, are a reflection of our own internal pollution, be it via thoughts, actions, food, drinks, toxic relationships, self-deceptions and so on.

Resistance to taking personal responsibility activates the fear matrix and victim consciousness can continue to thrive. This in turn plays into the self destructive nature of ignoring that we ourselves are part of the contributing factors to what is showing up in our bodies and on a larger scale, showing up on the planet. The misalignment between the external and inner realms does eventually manifest and create suffering somewhere. Walking our talk right here, right now allows the misalignment to diminish and dissolve.

It is time to become increasingly aware, mindful and informed about exactly what we are putting onto and into our bodies. And at the same time what we are subsequently putting onto and into the earth, the waterways, the oceans and the atmosphere. We are reflections of each other, the microcosm and the macrocosm, the human being and the planet earth.

Nature left to its own devices is diverse and everything finds its place. Nature controlled by man is manipulated and monoculture is encouraged, resulting in dependency on a few species, which can be wiped out in an instant. The selected few result in greater controls being instigated to protect them against nature, and that results in greater use of chemicals and manipulation, both of which impact upon the beings that consume them. Apples, potatoes, rice, bananas and tomatoes are some examples. Genetically modified (GM) crops require vast amounts of chemicals to protect them, and we later ingest those same chemicals.

Diversity however, has an in built system so that if one strain is affected, the others are not. Farmers know that and that is why they grow different varieties of the same crop. The mixes allow all to strengthen and thus supplies continue without the use of chemicals or manipulation. That in turn has a better and healthier impact on all who consume them, as well as, on the land and the planet as a whole. Why are we allowing laboratory scientists to tell us how to farm the land?

There is so much information available concerning the impact and effects of genetically modified crops that it is quite amazing that it is still allowed to be produced and sold. GM crops and the pesticides required to 'protect' them, affect all flora and fauna in a destructive way. An excellent well researched documentary *'All of us Guinea pigs Now'* directed by Jean Paul Jaud, clearly shows the detrimental and abusive results and as the film states *'This is the first time that technology can change the world entirely, giving the people who possess the technology power over the rest of the world.'* (Jaud 2012)

Two of the biggest biotech and seed bank companies, Monsanto and Syngenta, also produce agrochemicals, to enhance production of GMO food, which have been shown in scientific research, to cause harm to those who ingest it. They continue to do their upmost to silence all opposition. Apparently their influence around the world is linked to the financial investments they make in the political arena. Bayer, a pharmaceutical company, also produces hybrid seeds and pesticides under its wing Bayer Crop Science. It has reportedly brought legal proceedings against the European Union, for banning the pesticides it produces, which have been linked to killing bees.

These are interesting manifestations of the fear matrix at the corporate level. Bees ensure that pollination occurs and that means the natural cycles of all plants and crops continues. Killing the bees would give the seed bank companies ultimate control over food production.

Until we start to address our inner world and start to move through the fear matrix, toxic thoughts and limiting self beliefs, and begin to take personal responsibility for our lives and who we be, the outer world will continue to show up as the reflection of our relinquished responsibility and our victim consciousness. We shall continue to blame rather than change. We believe the world is coming at us. It is not. The world is actually coming from us.

It is also becoming clear, through research, that there are many medicines which exacerbate illness. It is important for each person to be mindful, to become better informed and to make their own choices about exactly what vaccines and treatments they actually wish to subject the body to, without being bullied into it through peer pressure or the threat of legal action. It is interesting that pharmaceutical corporations are attempting to patent and own all natural resources of plants and non chemical medicine. A giant conglomerate in business could be seen to be akin to a dictatorship in government, or a bully in the school playground.

The fossil fuels and the mining industries take precautions, yet sometimes there can still be seepage of vast quantities of toxins, onto the planet. We too are putting toxins, into our bodies in vast quantities when we consume processed, GMO and radiated foods, when we consume drinks in plastic bottles that contain PCBs, and when we eat largely manipulated and non digestible food. It is time to become better informed and to change how we do things in our own lives. We need to start looking at where we are polluting ourselves and why we are allowing it to happen. Which part of us feel is does not deserve? Which part of us feels others do not deserve? Why have we forgotten we are the Universe?

It is time to recognise and act upon the awareness that it is as important to build a sacred relationship with ourselves, as it is to develop one with Nature. We are one and the same. When I pick a flower as an offering or for decoration, I leave something of me with the plant. For example, I pull out a hair and place it on the plant. This serves to remind me of what I am taking from plants when I pick a flower.

People living within nature, are able to see at first hand, how their relationship with it affects nature and themselves. A garden or a plot of land that is cared for, appreciated and loved, thrives. One that is poisoned, criticised and abused, withers and produces little. Communities living within nature know that everything has energy. They know that everything is interlinked and interdependent. Have you noticed how peaceful parks and gardens can feel? Spend time in nature every day and feel the difference in how you feel.

Even if we live far from Nature, remember we are part of nature. We carry the essence of nature, presence and unconditional love, within us. Dropping into that, we too can hold space for ourselves and others.

Our oceans are dying. Radiation leaking into the Pacific, toxic wastes and all the plastic rubbish we generate are responsible for speeding up that process. Why is it that we as a collective, appear to allow governments to say yes to nuclear power plant developments and no to alternative power sources? The money needed to invest in a nuclear power plant is surely the same or more than needs to be invested into solar, wind or hydro power sources. To clean up nuclear waste is certainly more costly.

Small grass roots organizations, mainly in so called third world or developing countries, are having great success in providing solar electrical power for many of the poorest people. This happens in India. The technology has been developed because it had to be, as so many people are not covered by the multinationals. In parts of Peru clean water, collected from the condensation that forms on giant bill boards, is made available and is free for everyone.

A team at IBM recently developed and HCPVT system, a High Concentration Photo Voltaic Thermal, that is capable of concentrating the power of 2,000 suns. The process of trapping the sunlight produces water that can be used to produce filtered drinkable water. Scientists envision that the HCPVT system could provide sustainable energy and fresh water to communities all around the world.

There are currently people exploring the affect of sound frequencies and colour to restore health to large bodies of water, as well as, to people. There are possibilities arising every day, which can change the current reality we are experiencing and then imposing upon the future. A redistribution of research funds could result in different outcomes to toxic pollution and nuclear disasters.

When those that 'lead' have forgotten to address the day to day issues of life and focus on mega projects, it is a clear indication that we too have forgotten to address our inner world and our day to day living. This disconnection takes us so far from our true nature that we seem to have forgotten we have a voice. We also appear to have forgotten how to use it.

Even if we only use it within ourselves, within our internal dialogue to say to ourselves "I now choose to move beyond the matrix of fear and into the matrix of love," it is a start. When we can make that commitment to ourselves it will begin to assist us to decrease the number of toxic thoughts and the amounts of toxic foods we ingest every day. That commitment to ourselves will help us to find our voice and to step into our innate wisdom being. This being knows how to use its powerful voice for the good of all.

The impact of love on the body is visible to the eye, as well as, in the energetic field. Look at someone in love, they positively glow. This is easily seen within the physical body where everything is filled with vital energy. To be ourselves, bringing our awareness to what is imprinted and being held in the body, opens the way to more transformation.

There are an increasing number of books, films and studies being conducted concerning the effect of mental and emotional states upon the physical body. A few I have found most helpful, interesting and inspiring are; *Ask Anything, And Your Body Will Answer* by Julie J Nichols, Ph.D and Lansing Barrrett Gresham, *Heal your Body* by Louise L. Hay, *The Body is the Barometer of the Soul* by Annette Noontil and *The Secret Language of your Body* by Inna Segal. All of these books take a holistic approach and it's amazing what happens when you do that. *Molecules of Emotion* by Candace B. Pert Ph.D, substantiates these "knowings" with scientific observations.

A film called *What the Bleep Do We Know* explored this idea and had the main character imposing criticism upon her body. The work of Dr Masaru Emoto shows the effects of thought and intention upon water crystals, and as we are mainly water the effect is the same. Self acceptance, love and compassion given to the body can restore it to health.

Judgements, criticism, sticky love and attachment can have the opposite effect. If we store, hold onto and keep our past hurts, disappointment, anger, sadness, resentment, jealousies, and un-forgiveness, locked up in an eternal draw, it will impact on our physical body. The feelings have not gone away, they have simply festered and moved into a physical expression.

Physical conditions such as; cancer, poor circulation, irritable bowel syndrome, flu, skin conditions, asthma, a stiff neck, a frozen shoulder, diabetes and so on, all have a mental, emotional and spiritual quotient and reflect an "out of love" situation, belief and identity.

Whenever we wake up from sleep, a health restoring practice, we can extend gratitude and appreciation to our body and our heart. That heart which continues to beat, even when we are asleep. Compliment the body rather than judge it. Celebrate its incredibleness rather than criticise perceived flaws. Feed it nourishment and care for it as if was a newborn.

Treat the body kindly and you will be amazed at how it responds. All those perceived flaws melt gently and gradually away. Addressing the buried sources of disease may mean apologising frequently to your body for what you have allowed to fester deep within. As you do so, remember the principle of intelligent regret and move away from blame and guilt. Instead make up for lost time, and direct healthy self acceptance and compassion to the physical body.

This is love. There is a wonderful book *True Love* by Thich Nhat Hanh, and within it there are chapters addressing most aspects of life and relationships. There is one which especially addresses gratitude to the heart and the body. It is a book which can wonderfully transform our lives and in doing that, transform the lives of all those we are connected to. We have the power to change the interconnecting energetic web for all of us, by addressing ourselves, and taking some time each day to be in a state of appreciation or gratitude.

Changing our thought patterns changes us physically. Personal development work that we allow ourselves to do for, on and with ourselves, is a gift we give to ourselves and to others. It is not a wholly selfish act. When we operate from the heart and we step into a greater space of love, we give everything around us permission to do the same and this is such a delightful place to be.

"Love is an expression of the willingness to create space in which something can change." Resurfacing® (Palmer 1994, 90). This phrase applies just as much to ourselves as it does to others, and because everything starts and ends with us and our point of singularity, the sooner we start with us, the more rapidly we will experience something else.

In traversing the spiral of life and becoming ourselves, we will undoubtedly go through a lot of mud and gunk. It is not all sunshine and roses, far from it in fact. At times it is like the biggest worst storm, landslide and nightmare we could possibly dream up, and the irony is we have created it all. Wading through it, however long it may take, is committing to ourselves to be as authentic as can be.

This is a commitment to engage with life and with others. This is a gift like no other. It has no price, it has no beginning. We start exactly where we are right here, right now and continue on as we traverse the spiral of life. As we do so, with willingness, conscious awareness, and with our own presence, we will discover and reveal such jewels to ourselves, that our own version of Indra's net filled with diamonds, begins to light up our world. It will light up the world we experience. It is worth remembering that it is out of the mud that the lotus grows.

Life is an offering. Live it well.

Twenty

Death – Taking Flight

Death is the one thing we can be absolutely sure of happening at some point in our lives.

Death is a part of life. It is an opportunity for transformation and an opening into aliveness.

Life is fleeting.

What is this thing that all of us at some point just through being alive will experience? Why is something that is guaranteed, so guarded and so quietly spoken of? Why is it so often avoided and shied away from? Yet it is so very present in every moment.

Death is the elephant in the room. Everyone knows it is there, but no one talks about it, perpetuating the illusion or perhaps, in this case the delusion, that by doing so it will disappear. Perhaps it will become invisible, simply not exist and not happen to us. If perchance someone is daring or foolish enough to raise the topic and bring it to the room's attention, it will often be greeted with silence and then a change of topic.

To realise that nothing is fixed and nothing is permanent, is a way of preparing for the inevitable. To live life grateful that in this very moment we are alive, means we are beginning to realise that at some point we will die and not be here anymore. For those who wish to explore this further there are meditation practices on impermanence and others on gratitude.

My focus here is on how we respond to death, as the ones remaining after another has died and left the body. The death of a being close to us is a discombobulating experience. It does not matter if it is a person, an animal or indeed for some, a beloved tree. It throws into question the very essence of our own sense of mortality and being. It can at times feel like the rug has been pulled from right under our feet while we were busy somewhere else.

Every death of someone close, results in a cracking open of the heart space. As the heart breaks, the tears flow and the heart opens a little wider. It opens a little wider to receive an infusion of love.

When someone dies there is an activation of the heart. As painful as it maybe, we have an opportunity to keep the heart open in spite of it and to be, give and receive love unconditionally. We equally have an opportunity to shut it down completely and to bury the pain and our very essence along with it. The gift of another dying is this opening and activation of our heart.

In some cultures death is a rather taboo subject. In others it is outwardly honoured and respected by the community, yet internally people are left to themselves to navigate the surges of emotions, and states of being which ensue. In some cultures it is taboo to cry for different reasons. One because that would be holding the spirit back on its journey, and two simply because you don't show sadness as that would be seen as a sign of weakness in a public display. In other cultures, mourners wail as loudly as they can and beat their chests, as the way to express the honour and respect they have felt for the person who is now dead.

The death of a parent is an incredible thing. Fortunately I had spoken to my father on his birthday, a few minutes before boarding a plane two days earlier, while in an airport transit lounge. The conversation from my side was rushed as a result. A quick happy birthday and I love you and that was it. Life is so fleeting.

We never know when our last conversation with someone may be. It is a gift to be as present as we can be when we are with or talking to another. I miss my father. He shows up from time to time in dreams or through other people, even things. It can, at times, be most entertaining, at others it comes from left field and takes me into a reflective space. Grief is something which moves through us in its own way, at its own pace. Allowing it to do so is a gift we can give to ourselves.

Each death I have experienced has been different and there have been a few these last few years. I share this one, for it allowed me to step into more of myself.

I was on my way from Cambodia to Bali. I had been there for ten days working with clients, and my plan on returning home was to sit quietly and write. The Universe had other plans for me and the writing was to wait for another six months.

The initial response when I received the call about my father's stroke, was to appreciate that being over 10,000 miles away in the southern hemisphere, I may not make it back in time. I asked my brothers to tell my father that I was on my way and that it was ok if he needed to go before I got there. I felt the need to give him permission that it was ok to let go. A practical instinctual centre opened up, there was no fear, no panic, just a putting of things in order, organising the next flight out and packing a bag. I noticed how quiet and still everything had become in that moment.

I did realise however, that the stillness may not last and that at some point during the 18 hour flight, I just might crack up. My system responds well to vibrational medicine, so I called a homoeopathist friend for a remedy to ease, though not to block the arising feelings.

The first surge of anger came when the car arrived to take me to the ticket office and airport. It was neither the usual car nor the usual driver. The car was in a very poor state, rather like my father. I can see that on reflection now. The driver however was excellent, patient and present. Rather like the doctors making my father comfortable as he slipped away over the next twenty hours. I reigned myself in, the arising anger, disguising a feeling of teetering on the brink of some abyss and being helpless to make it all go away. I managed to keep that at bay until it came to paying for the ticket.

In Indonesia, where I happened to be, there is a requirement with foreign currency. It must be absolutely clean and that means not a mark on it from a bank stamp to a cashier's pen. The sequence of series which will be accepted at their true value depends on the newness of the bills. I had managed to secure the right series, and most of the bills were crisp and new. When I went to pay, the cashier started rejecting bills which didn't match the criteria, and asked for an extra three precent to actually accept them as payment.

Well this saw the fire ignite and the inner rage at feeling so utterly helpless, spill over at the apparent injustice of a system so arbitrary and seemingly unfair. Clearly the response to my outburst of anger was for all the money to be returned and the cashier walked away. I didn't know I had it in me and her reaction slapped me right back into being present. The cashier had been absolutely right to calmly hand back the money and walk away.

Fortunately the travel agent stepped in and managed somehow to secure my ticket with the money and yes the additional three precent. Clearly I was a long way from reaching any mastery over my emotions that day!

Then everything went quiet and I travelled back to the UK having a five hour stopover in Bangkok, wondering all the while if I'd make it back to see the unconscious, but technically still alive being, who was my father. I took a book on death and dying with me, remembering it helped when my uncle died earlier in the year.

At first, I could not bring myself to start reading it on the plane, nor could I watch the movies. After some food I finally went for a movie and promptly cried most of the way through. It was about a family and a child who had taken on the illness of his father, yet who really ony wanted his father back and to experience his love. The name of the film escapes me now but as happens, it allowed some small release of the immediate sadness and the homeopathic remedy was working well.

About an hour away from London, as the dawn started to light up the night sky, I felt it was time to begin reading *The Tibetan book of the Dead,* by Guru Rinpoche according to Karma-Lingpa.

I landed to the most beautiful clear sky. I was through immigration and had my bag in record time, the only hitch, no driver. There had been an accident on the motorway and for the first time ever, the taxi was late rather than early.

Interesting how last minute hitches come into play. Once on my way up the M40, heading directly to the hospital in Oxford, I marvelled at the crisp warm autumn day, a heat wave no less. It was just before 08:00a.m. on September 29th 2011. As I looked at the clear blue sky I whispered "head straight for the blue Daddy, go straight for the blue, don't stop at the white, just keep going straight for the blue."

What can only have been a minute or two later a message came through from my younger brother, telling me that my father's spirit had gone. He and my elder brother were also moving slowly through traffic, in an unusual tail back, occurring on that very day. My father, I would like to think, feeling that I was back in the country and that his three children would now all be together, felt it appropriate to leave in the quiet of that early morning on the most beautiful day. Ironically, he was usually late, and for once he was early and we therefore were late.

There is a stillness that comes from somewhere deep inside at that very moment. A detachment from all things routine and the urgency of daily matters seems somehow to vanish. There is a presence that comes with death, an acceptance that nothing can be changed and yet at the same time everything has changed.

The way we respond to death is highly individual and personal, yet there are some common elements that many of us experience. I share my experience in the wish to illuminate areas which seem all too frequently to be ignored, and so exacerbate our own feelings of being bereft and alone, when someone we love dies.

In some cultures after a death, there is a ritual washing of the body and everyone gathers around to tend to the spirit. In my case, the hospital staff took over once we had said and done what we felt to say and do. Each of us were holding space for the others, until we were all ready to take our leave.

We moved from the hospital to the registrar's office and the public offices to organise death certificates and such like. Amazing how organised one must be at such a time of transition and transformation. This movement, of course keeps the attention focused so that there is a falling to pieces without falling apart. Focusing the mind enables one to get on with the affairs of the dead, through the demands of the living.

The funeral home or house as they are frequently called, is the next place and again how surreal the hushed tones, the soft lighting and dimly lit meeting rooms, all seem to be. The bizarre nature of coffins, the incredible things you need to choose from and sort through, and the plans that need to be made to administer the proper laying to rest of the dead. It can take a long time for a funeral to take place in the UK. Unlike in parts of South East Asia where people's bodies are generally buried within a day, even if they are, months later exhumed for an elaborate and costly cremation, as happens in Bali.

With death comes not only anger and sadness, there can come relief, and there can also come the realisation that with death comes freedom. Freedom for the one who has died from what they may have been struggling with in their lives. Freedom within oneself also, as a sense of freedom from the presence of the being who has died, can arise.

As I observed the mixed emotions and sensations I experienced with and through my father's death, I was both in the experience and fortunate to have many tools in my conscious awareness, so that I could observe what I was experiencing at the same time.

This meant I was reflecting on it and doing my best to not get stuck or caught up in the stories, at least not for very long.

As time went on, the insights started to come. I realised that it was the little girl, the child who was crying over the death of her father. The adult was the one who felt relieved for him and could celebrate his life and his passing. The child however, was the one who felt lost on the one side and yet free to find herself on the other. My father was a very loving and charismatic man, yet he could also be tyrannical at times and caught up in his own stories. He was often absent in his presence, and as the first month since his death passed more realisations floated to the surface.

I was grieving over the loss of a relationship, the relationship with a parent and a loving father. However at a youngish age and certainly by ten, I was scared of my father and did not recall him being around so very much. When he was, it was frequently a battle field of words. Words can be equally effective in inflicting wounds.

As I looked at this fact versus fiction story floating in my field, I began to realise that I was in part crying over a relationship that I didn't feel I had had enough of, and on another level, that I didn't feel I had had at all. Now that my father was permanently absent, having exited from the physical world, I had no chance to have this longed for relationship with him. And yet, at the same time I was free from the imposing and frightening energy of my father.

The next piece arose one morning, when panic set in and I felt incredibly vulnerable. There were carpenters working on the neighbour's house. They were being friendly by saying hello and looking into my garden. I flew into the house, wishing to shut out the world and stop people from looking at me. I later appealed to the neighbour to say something to the carpenters, but we seemed to be speaking at odds and I could not convince him of his responsibility to protect me.

Again observing this and being with it at the same time meant I watched as the archetypes, and the beliefs associated with them, came into play from deep within the psyche. The father, who is on some level the male embodiment of All That Is, the King, the Warrior, the Lover and the Magician, is meant to protect his children.

My father's absence, through death, meant suddenly there was no one to protect me, even though my father had seemed to spend much of his time refuting my ideas and idealism, so that I had felt unprotected and unsupported by him in life.

Unravelling this piece led me to appreciate the anger that had arisen from being looked at. It was another piece of a puzzle. I had missed being seen for who I really was and I felt I had not actually fully existed in my life. Ironic that there I was asking my neighbour, who was indeed a father, simply not my father, to protect me, as if he were my father. At the same time through the vulnerability came the sense that now I was free to be myself. Now I could be seen. Such delightful contradictions and yet this is what so much of our life is, an intricate web of delightful contradictions.

Gently and gradually over time I have taken up myself and expanded into the space that has been created internally and externally through my father's death. The gifts he has given in his dying have been as manifold as the gifts he gave to me and so many others through his life. I found Family Constellation work to be a valuable part of reclaiming and disentangling myself, and finally making peace with the relationship I had with my father.

A death in the literal sense is letting go of the other and it requires an allowing of the identity associated with that other to go too. Part of us dissolves when someone close dies. We experience a metaphorical death creating space for something new to emerge. A birth occurs.

At times it felt like the part that was mourning was the part that was also dying and dissolving, which in many ways, metaphorically it was. Tuning into that part, is a key to making peace with, and being present with exactly where you are in relation to the one who has died. The following may help. Ask yourself

Who is it that feels bereft?

Which identity or identities?

What does it or do they need?

What does it feel it has lost?

Ask these questions repeatedly, each time a new stage arises. Trust and receive the answers that come, with compassion and with gratitude. Be aware that as you are now your own parent, it is now your responsibility, role and position, to give these parts of your mourning self, all the elements it needs.

Death is an incredible gift for it breaks the heart open. As the heart centre opens, everything softens. We can choose to keep it open or to shut it down. The opening of the heart centre allows love to flow. In death we are being given a gift of love.

The loss of someone dear can suddenly make us realise how our fear of loss has locked us up in a world so small and tight we could hardly move for fear. We hear so many people say "I am so sorry for your loss" and yet I haven't heard someone follow that with "I am so happy for your gain." With the going, is a coming and it requires being present with what is, to perceive that.

In some ways death and loss can be followed by a recklessness and abandonment of control, a letting down of all the walls and barriers built up over time. Miraculously the realisation dawns that all the thoughts and feelings we have been holding on to in our hearts have been out of fear of loss; loss of face - rejection, loss of connection - abandonment, loss of strength and protection - vulnerability, loss of importance - position and ordinariness. This fear of loss creates separation. It is imperative to drop the fear of loss, for it is only a perception. That perception changes depending on how we are viewing something and where we are viewing it from.

Fear of loss of face, connection, strength, protection, self-importance and position, are all ways that we restrict ourselves, from expressing the truth of who we be and what we feel. They are all ways in which we say no to love. "I will not say what I think in case I am wrong. I will not express how I feel in case it is not returned. I will not make the first move, in case I am ridiculed." And so on. These are all ways we isolate ourselves and build internal prisons, which keep the external world and our dreams so far away from us. It is not that they are not there. They simply cannot get past the walls we have built with our boulders of fear of loss.

A vital step to take when being present at another's death is to really be fully present. Birth and death are both a privilege to be present at. It is important to acknowledge to yourself and to the person dying, that they are in fact, dying. Do not lie about it. Give the person permission to go. It makes it so much more dignified and respectful. Dying is as sacred as birth. It is a going to be followed by a coming. Honour it, respect it and be present with it. Then savour the moments between the going and the coming. Take your time with all that is there, and do not be ashamed at the plethora of thoughts, feelings and sensations that you have. Be as present with them as you can be and gradually the emergence of what is coming will reveal itself to you.

We can all make that difference in the world, by beginning to honour the goings just as much as the comings. Let go of the fear of loss, one piece at a time and create more space in your world. The freedom you will experience and share with others, will encourage greater authenticity and presence in relationships, on all levels. That will also be reflected in the world that we experience on the outer, as well as, the inner realms.

May the birth begin.

Twenty-One

Birth - Coming into Land

Death and birth are inextricably linked
Birth is an ending of life inside the womb
Birth is a beginning of life outside the womb
Death is an ending of life outside the womb
Death is a beginning of life inside the womb
Birth and death are the outside and inside of life
Birth and death are the spiral of life
To be present and witness at a birth, how could we ever contemplate taking life?
To be present and witness at a death, how could we not contemplate giving life?
Yet both the birth and the death contain each other
As the baby is born its transcendental form slips into a physical manifestation of the energy of love, dying unto itself in the process
As the being passes through its physical manifestation of life into its transcendental form, it slips into an etheric manifestation of the energy of love, dying unto itself in the process
We move from the etheric into form and from form into the etheric
We move from oneness into form and from form into oneness
We move from expansion to contraction and contraction to expansion
We move from being limitless to limited, back to limitless once more
From water into water
From love into love

From etheric into form
From form into etheric
From pleasure through pain into pleasure free from pain
From infinite to finite, from finite back to infinite
We are all that is
All That Is, is what we be

Nicky Kassapian ©2012

Birth and death are such surreal events, it is little wonder so many of us are naturally born and die through the late hours of the night, or the first hours of the morning. We follow the natural rhythms of the body and creation. Through darkness into light, the sacred hours of birth and death. Through midnight and dawn, something sacred occurs.

It is an extraordinary privilege to witness a water birth and I was greatly moved when asked to attend the birth of my friends' son. The parents both being divers, were highly attuned to the potency of water. To be present at such a profound event between such respectful, loving and caring beings was a true gift. The couple were supportive all the way, seemingly carried on a solid wave of love. Both trusted fully the body's innate wisdom, strength and intelligence, to bring "love" into existence.

At one moment, just for a moment, fear entered the field and it was palatable. Everything went into reptilian brain, fight or flight, contraction and doubt. Power and strength were momentarily given over to another source, rather than trusting in the breath and the intrinsic nature of wisdom. Yet the antidote to fear, so instantaneously effective, was to come back to the breath, to come back inside the body, and to come back into the intrinsic nature of love.

Breathe in love, breathe out love. That is all we be and that is our guide to being all that we can be and to being all that we can become. The baby made his final exit from his mother's body with a rapid spiral twist into the water at 06.08a.m. He continues to navigate his spiral of life in physical human form.

There were many things that struck me afterwards. Even though none of us had had any sleep for twenty four hours, there was a sense of calmness and a clarity that followed. It was similar to the calmness and clarity that can follow a death. For me it was as if I was able to see more clearly into the heart of life. It left me wondering about the sense we have of ourselves.

How is it possible for any woman, who has given birth herself or been present at and witnessed the birth of another, to believe that she is powerless, weak, uselesss or not good enough?

How is it possible for a man who has been present at a birth, to believe that about a woman, or to believe it about himself either?

A woman is incredible and what her body can do is phenomenal. Such strength, power, grace, expansion and contraction, all called upon to bring forth life drenched in love. It is almost beyond words. This is something to be revered, respected, honoured, reclaimed and celebrated by women, by girls, as well as, by men and boys everywhere.

Men and boys have such a pivotal part to play. It is their contribution to the whole and their gentle strength, support and steadfastness, which can create the space for the tremors of life to be held, until the miracle of the newborn appears into the outer world. With the man at her back the woman can withstand the ripples of tumultuous pain, as he absorbs that which she passes through to him. Together they create a unified field, worthy of welcoming and holding this precious life, forming a spiral of baby, mother and father, as they die to who they used to be, giving birth to another and themselves.

Life is a gift and to treat it as such from the moment of inception to the moment of birth, and onwards through out life to the moment of death and beyond, is to honour our sacred origins and the miracle of that "collision of energy in space," which brought us into being. If we can start from this point, seeing ourselves as love, right here, right now, we can start to change the way we view and treat ourselves and others on the planet. It is that simple and it can be done.

Imagine all the people, breathe in love, breathe out love, breathe in love, breathe out love, breathe in love, and breathe out love.

The Universe is comprised of energy
We are microcosms of the universe
We too are comprised of energy
Recognizing that we are the convergent point of the energy in our lives
Places us in the optimum position to become
master of our own energy source

Nicky Kassapian © 2008

The Practices

A Extended Practice – Breathe in Love, Breathe out Love
B Daily Practices – Food for the Soul
C Evening Practices – Rest for the Spirit

An extended practice - Breathe in love, Breathe out love

The following practice, split into three parts is best enjoyed over a three week period. One part per week and it can be extended for a long as you wish.

The Practice

Part One - Try to do this at the same time each day, every day for one week.

A beautiful and very simple practice is to take a twenty minute walk. Be conscious of your breath, breathing in love, breathing out love, and as you walk start counting your steps. Count them slowly, gently and mentally without using a pedometer! Just be with yourself and with your feet. Bring your awareness to the motion of putting one foot in front of the other, for five minutes. This will bring about an altered perceptual state. It will bring you right back into your body and into direct connection with the earth. You will have experiential clarity as to where you have been or better still where you haven't been.

For the first few minutes or even steps, you may find yourself looking at your feet, as if seeing them for the very first time, and become more aware of their connection to the rest of your body. It can be quite something to suddenly have a flash of greater awareness of being in your body.

After a while you can walk and count without having to look at your feet, yet still have your attention on them as you look out into the world in which you are walking. You may notice, the sensation of an expanded state of awareness occurring. Take some additional time to enjoy it, for this is an aspect of consciousness becoming aware of itself as existence. This is the gift of you and it is space.

Part Two – Try to do this at the same time each day, every day for one week.

After a week of doing the conscious deliberate aware walking, breathing in love and breathing out love, and counting your steps, it is time to add another element. Rather like a walking meditation, each additional element will take you to another aspect of the perceptual field. In this part you will be widening and deepening your perceptual field

This is a gorgeous walk which I have adapted from Awakening The Will, *Resurfacing*® (Palmer 1994. 35) This time as you do your twenty minute walk, spend the first five minutes counting your steps as before. Then for the next fifteen minutes, as you walk, pick out something that you haven't really noticed before and stop to really look at it.

As you look at it, start to describe it to yourself in detail. If you can, do so without naming it. For example, it is tall, round and made of wood, it is light brown and beige with bits of cream and green on it, creating a mottled effect. It is about three meters tall and the main part of it is about 50cm in diameter. It divides into many other parts from the central sections and stretches up towards the sky. On the ends of the subsections are lots of small green, red and sometimes yellow objects, opening themselves to the sunlight and the elements which fall upon them from the sky...

Continue describing the object until there is nothing more that comes to mind. Then you place your attention back on your feet and breathing in love, breathing out love, take a few more conscious and deliberate counted steps, until you come across another object that attracts your attention, pause and describe it in detail. It may take longer to cover the same distance than when you are simply counting. This is to be expected. It is not the distance we are interested in, it is how you feel and how you perceive the world after you have completed your twenty minute daily practice.

You can, to my knowledge, expect that this time the perceptual shift maybe that the world appears brighter, clearer and more vibrant. Your ability to see depth and detail is sharpened. You may feel you are more present with your surroundings, and you may also have a greater sense of expanded awareness, and connection to the earth and your environment. These are just some of the things you may experience. There are many variations.

It doesn't take long to create space so that you can fall out of the head and into the heart.

Observe what comes up for you during the first two weeks. Notice the way you feel in the inner realms and what happens in your external life. Notice the thoughts and sensations that you have, just like someone watching a film, no need to go into them, understand them, or try to control them. Notice the people who show up in your life, observe the conversations you have. Enjoy the space you have created and allow yourself to continue to be mindful as you go through your days and nights.

Part Three – Try to do this at the same time each day, every day for one week.

In this third week you will add awareness of colour, to your walks.

For the first three days of the week take a twenty minute walk. Breathe in love, breathe out love and place your attention on your feet. Be aware of the motion in your body as you walk, counting your steps consciously and deliberately.

Notice objects of colour, and be with whatever it is, for a brief moment, noticing the texture, the form and the graduation of tones.

Is it a blanket of uniform colour? Is it there each day as you walk and does it look the same each time?

What impact does the change of light have upon it? Does it still attract you as before?

For the second half of the week, take a walk, preferably in a natural environment like a park or a garden, breathing in love, and breathing out love and stand in front of whatever colour it is that attracts you.

Take a few moments to familiarise yourself with the texture, shape and tones of the colour. Then gently and slowly breathe in the colour. Breathe it in lightly at first until you feel comfortable and then allow yourself to breathe it in more deeply if you wish.

Please note the experience may make you a little giddy even a little dizzy, so enjoy doing this slowly and only do one day.

When you have finished, return to observing something in your environment and describe it to yourself in detail. Then continue on your walk, breathing in love, breathing out love, consciously and deliberately counting the steps, putting your awareness on the environment around you.

This part of the practice will take you into the realm of colour and move you from the outside of the colour, to the inside of it. Then as you put your attention on an object and describe it in detail you expand that perceptual field once more and reconnect to the external environment. Finally with the walking, you are allowing yourself to be both present on the internal realms, inside the body, and at the same time, consciously experiencing the awareness of your connectedness to the external realms, outside the body.

You may find that the solidity of difference that you thought existed between the external and internal realms starts to soften, and the separation and sense of disconnection begin to diminish. There can be more space, more peace, more freedom, and more allowing of all things to be, as well as, more trust in yourself and in the world you are creating.

As we begin to look at, to sense and to perceive the environment around us in a more connected way, we in turn begin to look, sense and perceive ourselves in a more accepting, forgiving and compassionate way. We are creating the space where we can drop out of the head, full of preconceived ideas, and fall into the heart, supported and guided by the intuition. We can once more begin to be alive, feeling life with our three centres moving in harmony.

Daily Practices - Food for the Soul

Sky and Earth Meditation
Intentions
Gratitude and the Body
Gratitude and the World

The world is coming from us. Whatever we are seeing out there, is a reflection of what is going on inside us too. We can all rave, appreciate, point out and criticise, but until we start to recognise that it's all emanating from our own inside world, we will be doing little other than spending energy on things which are going nowhere fast. We will be perpetuating the inertia and feeding a matrix of fear, through the feelings of despair, hopelessness and poor me.

Taking a good look at where things are out of alignment within ourselves, means that we step into a different matrix. As we take ownership of our contribution to what we see outside, we are in turn making a difference and becoming a catalyst for creating the environment of greater alignment on the planet.

Right now, the most secure investment, the one that will give us and others, the greatest profits we can ever imagine, is the one we make in ourselves. As great teachers have said, "it pays to be consciously selfish." "Change yourself and the world changes." Simple and true.

So how to become the convergent point within our own world of dualities, creating a sacred place within from which all new worlds can emerge?

Firstly, we may want to contemplate the concept that there are few things which are constant in our lives. One is breath, two is you, and three is change. Breath is the bridge between the mind and the energy. When we change how we breathe, we change how the mind works and we improve our flow of energy. We are always with ourselves, even when we wish we weren't, we will find that we are.

Getting to know ourselves can be the journey of a lifetime or many.

Sky and Earth Meditation

The Practice

Reconnect to yourself and start with making quiet time just for you, each day. Five minutes is a beginning.

Sit for a moment, in silence and be with yourself.

Connect to the earth. Imagine roots coming out of your feet and extending down through the floor, the earth, the rocks, the water table, the sand, and the earth, until your roots have gone so deep you arrive at the centre of the earth.

Then allow your roots to spread out as far as they can go, in all directions. You now have a stable base to carry you through you day.

Coming back up to your feet, allow your attention and the energy of the earth, to travel up the length of your body to your head. Then send out a shoot, as far as it can go, up into the sky. Allow a canopy to expand out and fill every direction, just like a tree.

Inhale through your feet and through your head, and feel the two energies meeting in your heart.

Listen to what it tells you.

Take some time to be still in this space and when you are ready, set an intention for your day.

Include:

How you would like to be – *creative, present, kind, open, expressive.*

How you would like your day to unfold – *with grace and ease.*

What you would like to contribute to the outer world – *kindness.*

Walk through your day, as grounded as the earth and as open as the sky. Be guided by your heart. Keeping your eye on the bigger picture, means you can be flying high, safely anchored deep inside the earth.

Intentions

The Practice

A word on intentions, they can include how you are going to go about your day. They are not just about what you want to happen, what deals you want to conclude and so forth.

Ask yourself what kind of people you wish to encounter during your day.

Would your preference be helpful, calm, relaxed, dynamic, appreciative and peaceful ones? Or would you rather snappy, intolerant, demanding, ungracious, unforgiving and aggressive ones?

As you contemplate this, be aware that this is the type of person you must intend to be throughout your day too, so that you will also experience this.

As unpleasant as it may be to appreciate, the world is not only coming from us it is also a reflection of us. Owning whatever we are experiencing out there as actually coming from inside of us, is going to bring about major changes in the way we perceive and experience life, and how others will interact with us.

We are doing the whole planet a favour and changing what everyone experiences, and given the ripple effect, this encourages others to do the same.

Gratitude and the Body

Start your day connecting with the centre of the earth and the sky and set your intention for the day.

This means that you are grounded, anchored between the earth and the sky, and you can walk through your day, with your eyes on the bigger picture, guided by your heart and with your feet firmly on the ground.

You being this way, makes a difference for everyone you come into contact with. It is all about you.

The Practice

Take a few moments to connect with your physical body as you come out of the morning sky and earth meditation. Sit, stand or lay flat, whatever is most comfortable for you.

Bring your attention to your body, and starting from the toes all the way up to the top of your head, thank each and every part for making up your body and for what it helps you to do. Remember to thank your skin, muscles, tissues, blood, lymph, your organs and so forth. Thank every piece you can name, and then all the pieces you cannot name. Thank your heart and your lungs, your teeth, ears and eyes and so forth. Take as much time as you need to thank the whole of your physical body for creating the space so your spirit can experience the world though a more defined form. The body is on loan to us for this lifetime. Showing it gratitude helps it to support us better, and can improve our overall health and well being.

Slowly come back to the space and go about your day in a state of gratitude.

Now that you're moving with appreciation and gratitude, it's simple to take it a step further and really make a difference

Gratitude and the World

The Practice

Here's a fun, effective and easy way forwards, which you can do anywhere, anytime, no previous experience necessary.

I remembered this, early one morning as I sat down to enjoy a bowl of fruit for breakfast. I pressed pause and before I took a mouthful I decided to move into a space of appreciation and then dropped deeper into gratitude, for everything that had contributed to the end result – that bowl of fruit salad on the table before me.

You can do this towards anything or anyone. Everything has a connection to the sun and the earth, so this is where I suggest starting from. Adapt the example below to suit your own object of gratitude.

Take a few deep gentle breaths and drop into the heart space.

Start by appreciating and thanking the sun, the earth and the water.

Then focus on all the elements that have come into play to bring you what is in front of you.

For a bowl of fruit, the following steps unfold:

First I thank all the elements that enabled the fruit to grow, ripen and be succulent. I move on to the eco system, the trees, soil, water and insects, straight on to the fruit picker and the person who then took it to the market.

This involved a monetary side step, to extend gratitude to the people who had made the road, the people who had make the truck, the steel for the body, the miners for the ore, the rubber tappers for the tyres, the plastic for the component parts, the oil refineries, and all the people who work in that industry, the petrol attendant and the driver of the transport

Then back to the market and I extend gratitude to those who built the market space, those who mined the stone, excavated the sand to make the cement, and wove the baskets in which the fruit was stored.

I keep following the trail and thank the person who bought the fruit and prepared it. I remember to thank the knife and how that was produced to make the slicing of the fruit possible, so that it could finally be put into the bowl. Of course for the bowl, there's the potter to thank who made the bowl, and all the steps taken so that it could be placed on the table.

Once more I go back to the environment, to express gratitude to the trees, the loggers, the rivers, the boats, the boat crew, the carpenter, the furniture shop, and finally, the bowl full of fruit ready for me to eat breakfast with a spoon.

Now who and what contributed to making the spoon and the chair I was sitting on?

You get the idea by now I am sure.

This took all of eight minutes by the way, so don't even think about putting this in the "too hard basket" as my Australian friends would say.

You may of course wonder what this achieves, aside from a slower start to breakfast. Well do it yourself right now as you read this, for you can apply the practise to anything and you'll have your own experiential clarity.

You may just surprise yourself, as you begin to remember who you are, and who everyone else is, in relation to you and each other, as well as, in relation to the planet and what we are really doing here.

Appreciating just how interdependent our relationships are, changes the way we approach everything. Staying aware of this and acting accordingly, is part of our privilege and challenge this incarnation.

As more people step up to this and move through their lives in a greater state of appreciation and gratitude, the more fun and easy life will be for everyone. In turn the planet can redress the balance environmentally.

Evening Practices – Rest for the Spirit

Review and Dedicate
Naikan

Review and Dedicate

At the end of each day, put the day to rest before you go to bed and you will find that you sleep much better and wake up much clearer.

Before you begin, if you have been working a lot on a computer, with electronic devices or with a phone, then connect to the earth and release the charge in your body. You can do this easily by standing on the ground barefoot, with the intention to send all the energy to be safely grounded into the earth. If you live in an apartment and do not have a garden, get a small box, fill it with earth and stand in it. It will still work. Just remember to change it from time to time. Try it for a week and if it makes a difference continue. Get your own experiential clarity.

The Practice

Sit quietly for a few moments.

Begin to focus on your breath and connect with the core of the earth and the sky. Once you feel settled, start to review your day. See if you can recall everything that happened from the moment you got up, to the intention you set and onwards to what happened, in sequence, throughout your day.

Did you fulfil your intention?

What were the surprises of the day?

What was the happiest moment of the day?

What are the things that have been left unresolved?

Reflect on what you may have done to contribute the things that are not yet complete and what you can do to resolve them the following day. Send forgiveness to yourself and others if necessary.

What was completed?

Reflect on how that occurred and send gratitude to all who contributed to the completion, include yourself.

What were the three most unhelpful things that you did during the day? This is an opportunity to practice intelligent regret.

Offer them up for instant purification. There is no need to carry that weight with you through the night and into the following day.

Contemplate what action you could take to make amends, create a tentative intention, review it and do it when you embrace the next day.

What were the three most helpful things that you did during the day?

Offer them up in joyful celebration. Dedicate them towards the liberation from pain and suffering of yourself and others on the planet.

Alternatively you can dedicate them to someone specific in your life. Perhaps, someone experiencing a challenging time. For a more specific practice you can do the next practice.

Naikan

This is Japanese for "Inside Looking" or introspection. Naikan can be done regarding a specific person or organisation. It is especially recommended when facing challenges in relationships.

The Practice

What have I received from --------------?

What have I given to --------------------?

What troubles and difficulties have I caused to ---------------?

Close your evening with a moment in gratitude for the gifts of the day and take a few moments silence before going to bed.

Bibliography

Books

Braiker, Harriet B. *The Disease to Please: Curing the People-Pleasing Syndrome*. New York: McGraw-Hill. 2001.

Brown, Brene'. *Daring Greatly. How the Courage to Be Vulnerable Transforms the Way We Live, Love, Parent and Lead:* New York: Portfolio Penguin. 2012.

Botsman, Rachel, and Roo Rogers. *What's Mine is Yours: How Collaborative Consumption is Changing the Way we Live*. New York: Harper Business. 2010.

Chapman, Gary. *The 5 Languages of Love*. Chicago: Northfield Publishing. 2010.

Emoto, Masaru. *The Hidden Messages in Water*. New York: Atria Books. 2005.

Gibran, Kahlil. *The Prophet*. Oxford: Oneworld Publications. 1998.

Gottman, John M. *The Science of Trust*. New York: W.W Norton & Company. 2011.

Hanh, Thich Nhat. *True Love*. Boston, Massachusetts: Shambhala. 2006.

Hay, Louise L. *Heal your Body*. Carlsbad, California: Hay House Inc. 1988.

Kingsley, Charles. *The Water Babies*. London: Macmillan. 1863

Krishnamurti. *Freedom from the Known*. San Francisco: Harper. 1969.

Liedloff, Jean. *The Continuum Concept: In Search of Lost Happiness*. United States of America: DA CAPO Press. 1977.

Lim, Robin. *Placenta the Forgotten Chakra*. Bali, Indonesia: Half Angel Press. 2010.

Lipton, Bruce H. *Biology of Belief: Unleashing the Power of Consciousness, Matter & Miracles*. Santa Cruz, California: Mountain of Love. 2005.

McTaggart, Lynne. *The Field*. London: element, HarperCollins Publishers Ltd. 2003.

Moody, James Bradfield and Bianca Nogrady. *The Sixth Wave*. Australia: Random House. 2010.

Nichols, Julie J. and Lansing Barrett Gresham,. *Ask Anything And Your Body Will Answer*. United States of America: None Too Soon Publishing. 1999

Noontil, Annette. *The Body is the Barometer of the Soul*. Victoria, Australia: Self Published. 1994.

Odent, Michel. *The Scientification of Love*. London: Free Association Books. 2001.

Palmer, Harry. *Resurfacing®*. Florida, United States of America: Star's Edge International®. 1974.

Peirce, Penny. *The Intuitive Way*. New York: Atria Books/ Beyond Words. 2009.

Pert, Candace B. *Molecules of Emotion: The Science Behind Mind-Body Medicine*. New York: Simon & Schuster. 1999.

Rinpoche, Guru. According to Karma-Lingpa. *The Tibetan Book of the Dead*. Boston, Massachusetts: Pocket Book Shambhala. 1992.

Segal, Inna. *The Secret language of Your Body: The Essential Guide to Healing*. Victoria, Australia: Blue Angel Gallery. 1992.

Sills, Franklyn. *Being and Becoming: Psychodynamics, Buddhism, and the Origins of Selfhood*. Berkley, California: North Atlantic Books 2009

Steiner, Claude. *Scripts People Live*. New York: Grove Press. 1990.

Digital sources - websites, online videos and films

"Welcome to Avatar EPC" Avatarepc.com. Acessed November 13, 2013. www.avatarepc.com

"Adyasanti Events Satsang." Adyasanti.org Satsangs. Accessed November 10, 2013. https:/www.adyashanti.org/index.php?file=satsang

Beatrice'Camurat Jaud. *All of Us Guinea-Pigs Now. Mov* (online video September 22, 2012. *www.touscobages_lefilm.com*) https://www.youtube.com/watch?v=uznZEMeV7uA

"Somatopathie." Somatopathie.com. Accessed December 5, 2015. http://www.somatopathie.com/somatopathie/

"Sacred Economics." Sacred-economics.com. Accessed July 14, 2013. www.sacred-economics.com

"The Minimalists." Theminimalists.com. Accessed July 15, 2013. www.theminimalists.com

"The Resonance Project Foundation." TheResonanceProject.is. Accessed July 24, 2013. www.theresonanceproject.org

"The Venus Project." *Thevenusproject.com. accessed July 24, 2013.* *https://www.thevenusproject.com/zenhabits.net*

"Zen Habits." Zenhabits.net. Accessed July 15, 2013. www.zenhabits.net

Beatrice'Camurat Jaud. *All of Us Guinea-Pigs Now. Mov* (online video September 22, 2012. *www.touscobages_lefilm.com*) https://www.youtube.com/watch?v=uznZEMeV7uA

TheSystemsBuster. *Amazing Speech 1/3, 2/3, and 3/3 Jose Mujica President of Uruguay Speaks out at UN 2013.* (online vdeo, November 12, 2013) https://www.youtube.com/watch?v=OQ4a3zNbCFQ

Jeritadamsonfourman. *Nassim Haramein at the Rogue Valley (series)Metaphysical Library. 2003.* (online video April 22, 2011) https://www.youtube.com/watch?v=79_HwQ-92f8

Arntz, William. Betsy_Chasse and Mark Vicente, *What the Bleep do we Know.* (April 23, 2004. Phoneix, United States of America.) Movie.

About the Author

Nicky Kassapian, formerly a teacher, has developed her skills and expertise, as a healer and facilitator over the last three decades, working with individuals and groups worldwide. Nicky, based in South East Asia, is an artist and jewellery designer in her spare time.

www.nickykassapian.com

Printed in Singapore by Markono Print Media Pte Ltd